The Miss Dennis School of Writing

and Other Lessons from A Woman's Life

Alice Steinbach

The Bancroft Press
Baltimore, MD

This book is for my mother, in memory
And for my sons, Andrew and Samuel

Acknowledgments

Grateful acknowledgement is made to the Baltimore *Sun* for permission to reprint the following pieces, in whose pages they originally appeared from 1985 to 1995.

I would also like to thank my publisher, Bruce Bortz, and my editor, Connie Knox, for their counsel and support.

Above all, I am grateful to my family and friends without whom the life described in these pages would have been less complete. My heartfelt thanks go to my brother and sister-in-law, Shelby and Patricia Carter, who many times have come to my rescue, providing love and support. And, of course, words cannot convey what I owe to my sons, Andy and Sam, who continue to grace my life with their presence.

Contents

Introduction

From a shoebox of old postcards I lift one out — a view of Colette's grave in the famous Paris cemetery Pere Lachaise — and read the following message:

Dear Alice,

Traveling here on the Metro, I sat next to a young Frenchwoman holding a huge spray of flowers — pink roses, baby's breath, yellow lilies, all wrapped in clear, florist's paper that made crackling sounds each time the train leaned into a turn. By the time we reached Pere Lachaise, the entire metro car was filled with the scent of roses and lilies. It followed me all day and was waiting for me that evening when I returned to my hotel room. Falling asleep, I thought of my mother, of the Shalimar perfume she wore, of the way her clothes always seemed, at least to a small child, to smell of roses. You must try to remember this day, Alice: the day the scent of your childhood accompanied you, like a happy companion, through the winding paths of Pere Lachaise.

The postcard, dated June 1993, is signed: *Love, Alice.*

I first began sending postcards to myself about 15 years ago while on a trip to Bornholm, a small island in the Baltic Sea. I was traveling alone, tired and still reeling from the loss of an important figure in my life, when suddenly I succumbed to acute feelings of homesickness. By the second day of my stay, I found myself searching, like a sailor lost at sea, for something familiar, something to assuage my loneliness, and yearning for home.

Then one day, while walking along a road lined with fir trees, I came to an opening and found what I was looking for. There before me, bending to the wind, was a vast field of purple heather. Something inside me lifted and suddenly I was seeing the heather my Scottish grandmother lovingly described to me in the bedtime stories she wove about her life in Kirriemuir. "I have seen this before," I thought, standing there in the heather of Bornholm, watching as the unfamiliar slipped off its strangeness and took on the guise of an old friend.

2

That night I wrote my first postcard to myself, describing what I had seen that afternoon and what I had felt. When I returned to Baltimore, the postcard was waiting for me. I turned it over, read through it and came to the last line: "Try to remember this day: the heather, the wind, the peace that comes with knowing the familiar is everywhere."

In this book, I write about the familiar. It's taken a lifetime of learning to see that what has shaped me are not the lessons taught by the occasional encounter with the exotic moment. I take my form, instead, from the long, steady observation of the familiar; this is the force that has allowed me to see life whole and to make personal sense of it. It is this view that accounts for the recurring themes to be found in this book: family, friends, children, men, women, youth, aging, nature, home and, of course, cats.

What the reader will not find in these pages is the journalist's stance of distanced objectivity. Here, the third person gives way to the first. I learned early in my life, from reading the incomparable E.B. White, that a private experience, if deeply examined, can have universal value. "As a writing man," Mr. White observed in one of his essays, "I have always felt charged with the safekeeping of all unexpected items of worldly or unworldly enchantment, as though I might be held personally responsible if even a small one were to be lost."

In these pages, I have tried to rescue from insignificance some of the small events that make up a life. My hope is that such a recounting will evoke in the reader a personal response, one that causes a nod of the head in recognition or a sudden laugh at the familiarity of what's being described.

Finally, there is a ghost who haunts this book: Miss Dennis. It was she who helped shape my writing self, so much so that I have devoted the entire opening essay to her. Even now, I can't think of her without remembering her favorite words: "prairie" and "silver." She liked the sound of them, she said. It comes as no surprise that I've managed to work both words into these pages. Miss Dennis, I think, would have wanted it that way.

Baltimore
June 1996

The Miss Dennis School of Writing

W hat kind of writing do you do?" asked the novelist sitting to my left at a writer's luncheon.

"I work for a newspaper in Baltimore," he was told.

"Oh, did you go to journalism school?"

"Well, yes."

"Columbia?" he asked, invoking the name of the most prestigious journalism school in the country.

"Actually, no," I heard myself telling him. "I'm one of the lucky ones. I am a graduate of the Miss Dennis School of Writing."

Unimpressed, the novelist turned away. Clearly it was a credential that did not measure up to his standards. But why should it? He was not one of the lucky ones. He had never met Miss Dennis, my ninth-grade creative writing teacher, or had the good fortune to be her student. Which meant he had never experienced the sight of Miss Dennis chasing Dorothy Singer around the classroom, threatening her with a yardstick because Dorothy hadn't paid attention and her writing showed it.

"You want to be a writer?" Miss Dennis would yell, out of breath from all the running and yardstick-brandishing. "Then pay attention to what's going on around you. Connect! You are not Switzerland — neutral, aloof, uninvolved. Think Italy!"

Miss Dennis said things like that. If you had any sense, you wrote them down.

"I can't teach you how to write, but I can tell you how to look at things, how to pay attention," she would bark out at us, like a drill sergeant confronting a group of undisciplined, wet-behind-the-ears Marine recruits. To drive home her point, she had us take turns writing a description of what we saw on the way to school in the morning. Of course, you never knew which morning would be your turn, so — just to be on the safe side — you got into the habit of looking things over carefully every morning and making notes: "Saw a pot of red geraniums sitting in the sunlight on a white stucco porch; an orange-striped cat curled like a comma beneath a black van; a dark gray cloud scudding across a silver morning sky."

It's a lesson that I have returned to again and again throughout my writing career. To this day, I think of Miss Dennis whenever I write a certain kind of sentence. Or to be more precise, whenever I write a sentence that actually creates in words the picture I want readers to see.

Take, for instance, this sentence: Miss Dennis was a small, compact woman, about albatross height — or so it seemed to her students — with short, straight hair the color of apricots and huge eyeglasses that were always slipping down her nose.

Or this one: Miss Dennis always wore a variation of one outfit — a dark-colored, flared woolen skirt, a tailored white blouse, and a cardigan sweater, usually black, thrown over her shoulders and held together by a little pearl chain.

Can you see her? I can. And the image of her makes me smile. Still.

But it was not Miss Dennis' appearance or her unusual teaching method — which had a lot in common with an out-of-control terrier — that made her special. What set her apart was her deep commitment to liberating the individual writer in each student.

"What lies at the heart of good writing," she told us over and over again, "is the writer's ability to find his own unique voice. And then to use it to tell an interesting story." Somehow she made it clear that we were interesting people with interesting stories to tell. Most of us, of course, had never even known we had a story to tell, much less an interesting one. But soon the stories just started bubbling up from some inner wellspring.

Finding the material, however, was one thing; finding the individual voice was another.

Take me, for instance. I arrived in Miss Dennis's class trailing all sorts of literary baggage. My usual routine was to write like Colette on Monday, one of the Bronte sisters on Wednesday, and Mark Twain on Friday.

Right away, Miss Dennis knocked me off my high horse.

"Why are you telling other people's stories?" she challenged me, peering up into my face. (At 14, I was already four inches taller than Miss Dennis.) "You have your own stories to tell."

I was tremendously relieved to hear this and immediately proceeded to write like my idol, E.B. White. Miss Dennis, however, wasn't buying.

"How will you ever find out what you have to say if you keep trying to say what other people have already said?" was the way she dispensed with my E.B. White impersonation. By the third week of class, Miss Dennis knew my secret. She knew I was afraid — afraid to pay attention to my own inner voice for fear that when I finally heard it, it would have nothing to say.

What Miss Dennis told me — and I have carefully preserved these words because they were then, and are now, so very important to me — was this: "Don't be afraid to discover what you're saying in the act of saying it." Then, in her inimitably breezy and endearing way, she added: "Trust me on this one."

From the beginning, she made it clear to us that it was not "right" or "wrong" answers she was after. It was thinking.

"Don't be afraid to go out on a limb," she'd tell some poor kid struggling to reason his way through an essay on friendship or courage. And eventually — once we stopped being afraid that we'd be chopped off out there on that limb — we needed no encouragement to say what we thought. In fact, after the first month, I can't remember ever feeling afraid of failing in her class. Passing or failing didn't seem to be the point of what she was teaching.

Miss Dennis spent as much time, maybe more, pointing out what was right with our work as she did pointing out what was wrong. I can still hear her critiquing my best friend's incredibly florid essay on nature. "You are a very good observer of nature," she told the budding writer. "And if you just write what you see without thinking so much about adjectives and comparisons, we will see it through your attentive eyes."

By Thanksgiving vacation, I think we were all a little infatuated with Miss Dennis. And beyond that, infatuated with the way she made us feel about ourselves — that we were interesting people worth listening to.

I, of course, fancied having a special relationship with her. It was certainly special to me. And, to tell the truth, I knew she felt the same way.

The first time we acknowledged this was one day after class when I stayed behind to talk to her. I often did that and it seemed we talked about everything — from the latest films to the last issue of the *New Yorker*. The one thing we did not talk about was the sadness I still felt about my father's death. He had died a few years before and, although I did not know it then, I was still grieving his absence. Without knowing the details, Miss Dennis somehow picked up on my sadness. Maybe it was there in my writing. Looking back, I see now that, without my writing about it directly, my father's death hovered at the edges of all my stories.

But on this particular day, I found myself talking not about the movies or writing, but instead pouring out my feelings about the loss of my father. I shall never forget that late fall afternoon: the sound of the vanilla-colored blinds flap, flap, flapping in the still classroom; the sun falling in shafts through the windows, each ray illuminating tiny galaxies of chalk dust in the air; the smell of wet blackboards; the teacher, small with apricot-colored hair, listening intently to a young girl blurting out her grief. These memories are stored like vintage photographs in my memory.

The words that passed between the young girl and the attentive teacher are harder to recall. With this exception. "One day," Miss Dennis told me, "you will write about this. Maybe not directly. But you *will* write about it. And you will find that all this has made you a better writer and a stronger person."

After that day, it was like Miss Dennis and I shared something. We never talked again about my father, but spent most of our time discussing our mutual interests. We both loved poetry and discovered one afternoon that each of us regarded Emily Dickinson with something approaching idolatry. Right then and there, Miss Dennis gave me a crash course in why Emily Dickinson's poems worked. I can still hear her talking about the "spare, slanted beauty" in Dickinson's unique choice of words. She also told me that, despite the rather cloistered life led by this New England spinster, Emily Dickinson knew the world as few others did. "She found her world within the word" is the way I remember Miss Dennis putting it. Of course, I could be making that part up.

That night, propped up in bed reading Emily Dickinson's poetry, I wondered if Miss Dennis, a spinster herself, identified in some way with the woman who wrote:

"*Wild Nights — Wild Nights!*
Were I with thee
Wild Nights should be
Our luxury!"

It seems strange, I know, but I never really knew anything about Miss Dennis's life outside of the classroom. Oh, once she confided in me that the initial "M" in her name stood for Mildred. And I was surprised when I passed by the teachers' lounge one day and saw her smoking a cigarette, one placed in a long, silver cigarette holder. It seemed an exceedingly sophisticated thing to do and it struck me then that she might be more worldly than I had previously thought.

9

But I didn't know how she spent her time or what she wanted from life or anything like that. And I never really wondered about it. Once I remember talking to some friends about her age. We guessed somewhere around 50 — which seemed really old to us. In reality, Miss Dennis was around 40.

It was Miss Dennis, by the way, who encouraged me to enter some writing contests. To my surprise, I took first place in a couple of them. Of course, taking first place is easy. What's hard is being rejected. But Miss Dennis helped me with that, too, citing all the examples of famous writers who'd been rejected time and time again. "Do you know what they told George Orwell when they rejected 'Animal Farm'?" she would ask me. Then without waiting for a reply, she'd answer her own question: "The publisher told him, 'It is impossible to sell animal stories in the U.S.A.' "

When I left her class at the end of the year, Miss Dennis gave me a present: a book of poems by Emily Dickinson. I have it still. The spine is cracked and the front cover almost gone, but the inscription remains. On the inside flyleaf, in her perfect Palmer Method handwriting, she had written: "Say what you see. Yours in Emily Dickinson, Miss Dennis."

She had also placed little checks next to two or three poems. I took this to mean she thought they contained a special message for me. One of those checked began this way:

> Hope is the thing with feathers
> That perches in the soul ...

I can remember carefully copying out these lines onto a sheet of paper, one which I carried around in my handbag for almost a year. But time passed, the handbag fell apart, and who knows what happened to the yellowing piece of paper with the words about hope.

The years went by. Other schools and other teachers came and went in my life. But one thing remained constant: My struggle to pay attention to my own inner life; to hear a voice that I would recognize finally as my own. Not only in my writing but in my life.

Only recently, I learned that Miss Dennis had died at the age of 50. When I heard this, it occurred to me that her life was close to being over when I met her. Neither of us knew this, of course. Or at least I didn't. But lately I've wondered if she knew something that day we talked about sadness and my father's death. "Write about it," she said. "It will help you."

And now, reading over these few observations, I think of Miss Dennis. But not with sadness. Actually, thinking of Miss Dennis makes me smile. I think of her and see, with marked clarity, a small, compact woman with apricot-colored hair. She is with a young girl and she is saying something.

She is saying: Pay attention. ⊕

ALICE STEINBACH

Women and Men

13

When I was a teenager, most of what I knew about women and men I learned from three sources: Ernest Hemingway, Dorothy Parker, and my Aunt Claire.

From Hemingway, I learned that men are brave and fine and good and true. And that two of their main pleasures in life are bullfighting and drinking wine out of goatskins while speaking in terse sentences.

From Parker, I learned that women live their lives waiting for men: waiting for them to come home or waiting for them to telephone or waiting for them to propose marriage or to jump ship.

And from my Aunt Claire, I learned my most important lesson: to regard all such generalizations about women and men with a healthy dose of skepticism.

My Aunt Claire, who was the first truly independent woman I ever met, died a few decades before the arrival of such Wild Men and New Women as Robert Bly and Camille Paglia and the ensuing glut of books and televison talk shows devoted to the unbearable oddness of the opposite sex.

Still, it seems to me, most men and women are willing to attempt crossing the sometimes stormy waters of the gender gulf, knowing that on the other side lies something worth reaching: a shared humanity.

14

My Old Flame

We met for dinner, the two of us, in a small, Italian restaurant near his hotel. It was a reunion of sorts. Once, we had come close to marriage; he had proposed and I had accepted. That part I remember quite clearly. What has become less clear to me over the years is why our plans fell apart.

Since then, we've lived separate lives in different cities. But over the years, news filtered back to me: He was married; he was successful; he was divorced. Then one day the phone rang. He was coming to town. Could we have dinner?

I hesitated. In my head I quickly ran through all the reasons for avoiding a reunion with an old flame — not the least of which is disappointment; you with him, or worse yet, the other way around. But the simple fact is that all such reasoning gives way when that most demanding of all human needs kicks in: curiosity.

You find yourself wondering: What does he look like? How has life changed him? Will I see in him what I saw in him? Will I still find him attractive? And, more important, will he still find me attractive?

I agreed to meet him.

I dressed carefully for the occasion — which is to say I went out of my way to look good. Driving to the restaurant, I worked at retrieving the relationship, summoning up a kind of Cliffs Notes of memories: I tried to recall key feelings and events which outlined the way we were. It proved difficult.

It reminded me of a woman in one of Alice Munro's short stories: Thinking about a past and passionate romance, the woman realizes how distant and exotic the relationship now seems, thinking it was as if she "had once gone in for sky-diving."

I braced myself against the possibility that what once was so familiar to me would now seem foreign; remote; something that happened not to me but to another person.

But I needn't have worried. The old familiarity returned quickly and the evening was wonderful. Good company, good memories, good wine and, finally, goodbye — after years of occasional daydreaming — to any feelings I had of wondering, *What if … ?*

Whatever the reasons were for ending the relationship — the ones I no longer can remember — the evening ended with a feeling of closure. A benevolent sort of closure, though; one which allowed the past I shared with this man to exist again, restored to its proper importance in my memory.

Later, driving home alone, I turned on the radio. Some guy was singing: "If I knew then what I know now …"

It seemed a perfect coda — cliche though it was — to an evening which had involved the settling of some old accounts; accounts run up and unpaid for by a younger, less supple me.

What, I thought, would I have done differently in my 20s and 30s if I had known then what I know now?

Well, for one thing, I would have laughed more; seen more Laurel and Hardy movies. I would have been more spontaneous.

And I would have grieved less. I would have understood earlier that not all losses are permanent and that some things lost are not worth keeping.

I would have taken more time to note the changing seasons. ("Can you believe it?" an elderly friend asked me one spring day as we sat in her garden admiring the unfolding trees and flowers. "Can you believe that even if I live to be a hundred, I will see all this only 100 times?")

And if I had known then what I know now, I would have had more children. At least one more, anyway. Perhaps two.

I would have been more daring. Emotionally daring, that is; in the spirit of Eudora Welty's observation that "All serious daring starts from within."

I would have talked less. And I would have listened more. Especially to my children when they were younger.

I would have understood sooner how profoundly satisfying the ordinary transactions of daily life can be: the perfect cup of morning coffee; the son shouting down "Good night!" from his room; the ginger-colored cat caught napping in a triangle of sunlight.

Some philosopher — Kierkegaard, I think — pointed out that life can only be understood backward but must be lived forward.

True enough. But the direction you choose to take in going forward with your life can depend a lot on understanding where you've been.

And remembering who was there with you at the time.   ⊕

17

Fathers

Occasionally, when I'm walking down the street, I'll spot a man and think: He looks like my father.

I'm never quite sure what it is in these men that reminds me of my father. A tilt of the head, perhaps. Or a slightly amused expression around the eyes. Someone, perhaps, who telegraphs a sense of pleasure about the state of being alive.

One reason for my uncertainty about identifying the similarities between such men and my father is that I don't have a clear memory of what my father looked like.

Even now, when I study old photographs of him, I can't always connect my father with the young man captured so long ago through the lens of someone's camera. In China, the man in the picture sits in a rickshaw. In India, he's patting an elephant's trunk. In Rio de Janeiro, he's standing near the top of Sugar Loaf Mountain.

Still, there is one constant element present in all the men who remind me of my father: They're young. Or at least younger than I am. Somewhere in their mid-to-late 30s. The age my father was when he died just before my ninth birthday.

He was an adventurer, the man I knew as my father. Although he had a couple of college degrees and had taught at a university before my brother and I were born, it was not the life he wanted. His love of the sea and of the places it could take him drove him to maritime school. And then to a life at sea.

His family and friends — some of them, anyway — didn't understand the life he chose. His brothers — my uncles — never stopped trying to talk him into joining them in the family business. My father always listened politely — before politely declining the offer.

I guess if I counted up the actual number of days I spent with my father it would amount to the equivalent of a year and a half. He'd be gone for three or four months, then home for two or three weeks, then gone again. It was actually kind of exciting. When he was gone, there was always the anticipation — and the preparation — that revolved around his return.

To a child whose knowledge of future time was limited to getting up in the morning and thinking only about the day directly ahead, my father's appearances were wonderful surprises. He'd just show up. Or so it seemed to me.

But what I remember most about his appearances at home is the sense of presence he brought with him. Of being fully there, engaged in every minute of the time we spent together as a family. And, of course, it was always like a holiday when my father was home. Real life was banished.

Sometimes he'd take my brother and me on a tour of his ship. In fact, one of the most vivid memories I have revolves around finding a typewriter in my father's cabin.

I knew my father typed because the weekly letters he sent us were always neatly typewritten. What I didn't know, until that day, was that he also used that typewriter to type out the short stories he wrote. They were adventure stories, he told me. Stories set in the West in places with exotic names: Durango, Bitter Creek, Silver Bow, Laramie.

19

It was exciting to me, discovering — along with the typewriter — this new facet of my father. Sometimes, when I wonder in what ways he influenced my life, I think of that day: my father's excitement about writing and my dazzled receptiveness to his excitement.

I wish I could remember the last time I saw my father. The last time I said goodbye. The last time he held me. The last Father's Day we spent together. But I can't.

After all, why would I note such things? I expected them to go on forever.

Instead, on a hot June day, word came that he was dead. Somewhere off the coast of South America, he had drowned. His body was never recovered; it went with his spirit.

I have a theory that women like me — which is to say, women who had fathers for only a short time — never really give up the search to have back what was lost.

We search the faces of our sons, our brothers, our lovers and husbands, and even the occasional man on the street, looking for something, some trace of the lost father: a tilt of the head, perhaps. Or a certain expression around the eyes.

And sometimes we stop and wonder — although not often because it's too dangerous: If my father were alive, what would he think of me? Would he like me? Would he respect me? Would we be close?

I remember once, on a bitterly cold day in the seventh year of my life, my father suddenly showed up at my school. Although there was an hour to go before school was out, he talked my teacher into letting me leave early.

Outside it was so cold that the frozen ground hurt right through my shoes. But I didn't care: What I felt was happiness. I like to think he felt it too.

He Said, She Said

A few days ago, as I was sitting in a mall drinking a cup of fake cappuccino, I overheard a conversation between a man and a woman that went something like this:

"Do you think they're happy?" asked the young woman.

"Why wouldn't they be?" he replied. "Besides, it's none of your business."

"Don't be that way," she said.

"What way? I'm not being any way."

"OK. OK. I'm sorry I brought the whole thing up."

I found this conversation particularly interesting because I had recently finished a book called, *You Just Don't Understand: Men and Women in Conversation.* It was written by Deborah Tannen, a linguistics professor. It contends that women talk to create intimacy, while men talk to maintain independence and their competitive place in the world.

It's a natural progression from childhood, she maintains; a continuation of the different ways in which girls and boys learn to communicate. But it can cause serious problems in adulthood when messages get transmitted between men and women who are operating on different frequencies.

We would all be better off, in her opinion, if we could resist blaming one another for such breakdowns in communication, seeing them instead for what they are: cross-cultural differences between the sexes.

In theory, this No Fault approach sounds good to me. But in practice, I'm convinced it will never work.

Almost every woman I know — single or married — still asks the judgmental question: "Why can't a man be more like a woman?"

Linguistically speaking, that is.

Of course, all women know that men are capable of talking intimately. And at length. Is there any woman past the age of adolescence who doesn't remember those long phone calls from the Boyfriend? The kind of conversations that lasted for hours, ending only when your father threatened to rip the phone out of the wall and send you to a convent.

"Ah yes," observed a friend of mine when I reminded her of this kind of marathon phone talking. "Men do seem to talk during the Pursuit, don't they?"

Snide but true. On the other hand, it would be less than fair to skip over the fact that the way women *listen* to what men say accounts for some of the problems in communication between the sexes.

During the Pursuit, for instance, women tend to consider anything the Boyfriend says as fascinating, brilliant, and fraught with intimacy. "I like your hair that way," a boy once told me when I was 15 and wore my hair in a ponytail. I spent the next week dreaming about whether he and I should marry right away or wait a year or two.

Of course, no one had a better ear for the verbal differences between men and women than the late, great writer, Dorothy Parker.

Listen:

"Do you want me to go out and get you some cigarettes?" he said.

"Goodness," she said. "If you want to go so much, please don't feel you have to stay."

"You've been funny all evening," he said. "Hardly said a word to me."

"I'm terribly sorry you haven't been having a good time," she said. "For goodness' sakes, don't feel you have to stay here and be bored. I'm sure there are millions of places you could be having a lot more fun." Ring any bells?

But now, let's go to some real people for the last word. Here's what two attractive singles told me about the way men and women talk:

The man: "I don't know what other men think — men don't talk about these things — but I despise relationship babble over all other forms of babble. Women love it."

The woman: "I have never, I swear to God, asked a man to talk about our relationship. I do, however, think women need more verbal information about what he's thinking than men need."

The man: "You wanna know the worst feeling in the world? You're happy and content and having a nice time and the woman you're with announces that she wants to talk. You're trapped. No matter how hard you try, you know at some point you're going to make a mistake."

The woman: "I have been astonished to hear a man say something profoundly tender in the most offhand way. You know:

'You're beautiful.' Or 'I think about you all the time.' Or 'I told my sister I was in love.' I invariably say: 'I am? You do? You are?' I'm always surprised because it seems so sudden."

He said. She said. Some things never change. And the sooner we accept this, the better off we'll all be. ⊕

23

My Funny Valentine

The assault begins when I go to the drugstore. There they are, everywhere: rack after rack of glossy Valentine cards and big, heart-shaped boxes of candy.

I open the newspaper and there they are: page after page of advertisements for heart-shaped diamond pendants, a romantic dinner for two, and a dozen long-stemmed roses delivered by a kid dressed as Cupid.

I turn on the radio and it's all I hear: the sounds of "Endless Love" and "When a Man Loves a Woman" and "We've Only Just Begun."

Yes, dear reader, as Valentine's Day fast approaches, they're playing songs of love.

But not for me.

Right now, it's not looking so good for yours truly in the hearts and flowers department. Who was it who said that Valentine's Day is the cruelest holiday of them all, mixing memory and desire? Elton John? Merv Griffin? Oprah Winfrey?

And who was it who wrote:

"Oh, life is a glorious cycle of song,
A medley of extemporanea;
And love is a thing that can never go wrong;
And I am Marie of Roumania."

Why, Dorothy Parker wrote that, of course. The same Dorothy Parker who described herself, when it came to affairs of the heart, as "the greatest little hoper in the world."

Sometimes, however, hope is not enough.

That's when memory kicks in to fill the vacuum. Temporarily, one hopes.

So. Here I am on a Saturday night, sitting alone in my bathrobe and trying to remember the best Valentine's Day I ever had.

Actually, it was two. You see, I got engaged on Valentine's Day. Twice.

Once to my ex-husband. And once to my ex-fiance. (Ex, you might say, marks the spot in my life — romantically speaking.)

I remember both engagements as quite romantic, although I should warn you that my memory may be failing or, worse yet, overcompensating. One engagement took place in a blizzard; the other on a tropical island. Which leads me to speculate — with no scientific foundation, of course, for such a thesis — that extreme weather may play a role in matrimonial decisions.

(*Note to travel agents and cruise line operators:* For a slight fee, I would be happy to appear in ads for cruises to Alaska or the Caribbean, testifying to the above benefits of travel, marriage, romance, etc., etc.)

And speaking of travel, such thoughts lead me back to the memory of the worst Valentine's Day of my life.

I was 13 years old; the boy I coveted was Jerry Lizt. Jerry was my older brother's friend and scarcely knew I existed. But after months of screwball plans at getting noticed (I won't go into details, but one scheme involved a complicated falling-off-the-glider-and-onto-Jerry's-lap trick), Jerry asked me to go to an ice hockey game on Valentine's Day. So far, so

25

good. Right?

How was I to know that Bunny Stubbs was going to show up in a short ice-skating skirt and blue angora sweater — the kind of sweater that, if you were built right, made you the Pied Piper to 16-year-old boys?

I cried for three days. A reaction which prompted my mother to remind me that "beauty is as beauty does." However, my Aunt Claire — a most sophisticated woman who lived in a hotel and wore fresh violets pinned to her fur coat — reacted somewhat differently.

She took me to Elizabeth Arden's Salon for a complete beauty makeover. Unfortunately, when we got home, my mother made me wash the henna out of my hair and lose the push-up bra. Then she said something like: "If someone's going to love you, don't you want it to be you they love?"

Just for the record, my Aunt Claire countered with something like: "It doesn't really matter who you love when you marry, because the next morning you're going to wake up and find out it's someone else."

I, of course, agree with them both. Recognition: it's what we're all looking for in the eyes of a new lover, isn't it? The look that says, "I know who you are. And I like what I see."

But most of us are a bit intimidated at the thought of shedding our outer layer of defense to expose the tender skin beneath.

But what the heck. I'm going to place one of those "Personals" ads in a magazine. And I'm going to be brutally honest about myself. It will read: "TEBSQICSVANBF (tall, extremely beautiful, slim, quite intelligent, confident, successful, very athletic, naturally blonde female) seeking same in man. Must be willing to travel to Alaska or the Caribbean." ⊕

Crossing the Gender Gap

My 22-year-old son, a liberated sort of guy who's been cooking since the age of eight, called from Japan the other day with an urgent request: "Mom, I'm having people over for dinner and I need your recipe for barbecued chicken." He paused. "And Aunt Pat's recipe for eggnog."

He was rustling up this slightly weird combination of food and drink, he told me, for Japanese friends who had expressed an interest in these two "all-American" dishes. It wasn't an unusual request. Last month I sent him my recipe for apple pie.

Later that week, I received a phone call from my other son, a student in Colorado. A liberated sort of guy who's been sewing and mending things like climbing equipment and down parkas since he was 12, this son wanted my advice about sewing machines: "What's a fair price for a second-hand sewing machine?" he asked.

This is the same son, incidentally, who for years begged me to teach him how to iron shirts. I always refused, afraid that, if I gave up all my "mother-type" domestic skills, my sons would not need me.

It's funny. When I realized I was never going to have a daughter,

I grieved a little over what I thought I was going to miss: the pleasure of sharing "womanly" things, things like cooking and sewing and gardening, with another "woman."

And I feared missing the kind of deep intimacy that, as a daughter, I had shared with my own mother. I knew I could love my sons deeply — but identify with them? I wasn't so sure. I grew up with an older brother and the gender gap between us remained too wide to cross.

In fact, by the time I reached motherhood, I had bought into the stereotype that the emotional reactions of boys and girls were completely different. And that I would never be able to identify with my sons.

But time — and my sons — proved me wrong.

As the mother of sons, I have come to understand that boys are just as vulnerable as girls to all the emotions that define the human condition. Feelings of love, friendship, rejection, ambition, insecurity, envy, generosity, anger, tenderness, self-esteem, lack of self-esteem — these are not gender-specific feelings.

I have watched my sons' pursuit of love and friendship and the need to belong. And once you have watched a son fight his way through feelings of sadness or rejection over the loss of a friend, the failure of a romantic relationship, the disappointment at being left out of some desired event, you soon understand that some things transcend gender identity.

It's been said that many men become feminists when they have daughters — that as the father of a daughter, they truly grasp, for the first time, the limitations placed on women by gender barriers. And there are few fathers who do not wish for their daughters the same opportunities in the world as they do for their sons.

But being the mother of sons is a consciousness-raising experience, too. And one of the things it teaches you is that while there are many differences between the way boys and girls view the world — and the way the world views them — there are also many similarities.

I know what it's like to be a woman. But being the mother of sons offered me a singular glimpse into what it's like to be a man.

Humorist Russell Baker once observed that the "three absolute requirements ... to qualify for 'man' status" in our society are "utter fearlessness, zest for combat, indifference to pain." Given such requirements, Baker added, he would have to consider himself "only a second-rate man."

What he's describing, of course, is part of the "macho myth." And just as the "feminine mystique" forced confining standards on women, so too does the "macho myth" force many men to feel "second-rate" if they don't measure up to that confining view of manhood. Both concepts also add to the suspicions with which men and women regard one another.

Over the years, as I've watched and listened and shared my sons' lives, I found there was not a lot — emotionally speaking — that I couldn't identify with. All I needed to do was summon up my own feelings from the past when something similar happened to me.

Of course, it was a wonderful bonus when my sons expressed an interest in such things as cooking or gardening — things I thought I could share only with a daughter.

On my most self-confident days, I like to think my sons have learned something from me about what it's like to be a woman. But mostly I'm grateful to them for allowing me to witness day by day, year by year, the unfolding of the boy into the man. ⊕

29

Romance

Quick," I say to a colleague, "what's the most romantic thing that ever happened to you?"

Her answer comes back with the speed of an arrow shot from Cupid's bow.

"This may sound really ridiculous," she says, "but I think it was when a guy I was dating kissed me while I was brushing my teeth. He had been away on a trip and rushed over to my house when he returned. He barged into the bathroom, said he was so happy to see me, and started kissing me — even though I had a mouthful of Crest."

Hmmmmmm.

"Quick," I say to another friend, "what's the most romantic thing that ever happened to you?"

He has to think for a minute. "I'd say it was the night my girlfriend climbed up a tree to rescue my kitten. I'm afraid of heights and was standing at the bottom of the tree looking up at this helpless, meowing kitten when my girlfriend simply leaped onto the lowest branch and worked her way up from there. And she hates cats."

Hmmmmmm.

One more time: "Quick," I say to a third friend, "what's the most romantic thing ..."

"I think it was when my wife started carrying my luggage on trips. I never asked her to do this, but I have a bad back and one time when we arrived at the airport, she saw I was uncomfortable and just picked up my suitcase. Does it all the time now."

Hmmmmmm.

Excuse me. But do you find something wrong with these tales of romance? What ever happened to the kind of Romance that went something like this:

"Our eyes met and locked in a fierce embrace. 'Guido,' I murmured. 'Guido.' The moon shone down on the 8-karat diamond ring he had just slipped on my finger. He kissed me. Someone was singing, 'Some Enchanted Evening ...'

He kissed me again. 'Guido, Guido,' I sighed. He picked me up in his arms and ..."

Well, you get the drift.

I'm trying to figure out just when Romance became romance. Trying to locate the moment in history when an intensely romantic involvement began to take on the coloration of a mild neurosis. Something to be cured by a mental health expert or a self-help book entitled, perhaps, "Why Do I Feel I Am Nothing Without Romance?" Or "Co-Dependents Who Are Too Romantic For Their Own Good."

Did Romance start going down the tubes when barber shops merged with beauty shops and became unisex hair cutteries where everybody could watch everybody else getting their hair cut, permed and dyed?

Or could the demise of Romance be traced back to the emergence of male strippers — such as the Chippendales — as the featured entertainers at bridal showers?

Oh. Here's one: Did Romance diminish a little with the advent of His and Hers sweatsuits?

I don't know. All I know is that believing in romance used to be easier. Sure, it's probably "healthier" to give up looking for Mr. Right and settle for Mr. Half-Right-with-Potential, but I tell you, a little Big Romance now and then can do wonders for your soul. Not to mention your complexion.

Speaking of which, I recently ran across this letter to *Playboy*. Signed "R.S. in Houston," the letter asked this romantic question regarding the perfect bedroom atmosphere:

"Dear Playboy, I would like to create as different an environment as possible. I'm thinking that maybe a fog machine stashed under the bed or in the closet would be a good addition. How practical is it?"

Playboy's answer?

"Dear R.S., You could probably pick up a fog machine from a heavy-metal band, but unless you want to turn your boudoir into a theme park, you should hold the special effects."

Wrong, *Playboy*, wrong! What *Playboy* is overlooking, of course, is that a little fog makes everybody look better. Romantically speaking. Sad to say, but there are very few of us who don't look better when we're a little blurred.

This brings to mind one of my own, personal, most romantic moments. It happened when I wasn't wearing my glasses and seated myself in a darkened theater one night next to a man I assumed to be my date. "Hello, sweetheart," I said, kissing him on the cheek. He took my hand and looked full into my face, brushing the hair back from my eyes. "Hello, darling," said the handsome stranger beside me.

I've never found out his name, and don't want to know. It would break the spell. Although he looked like a Guido to me. ⊕

Women and Confusion

For the past year, I have kept under my desk at home a large card-board box labeled: "Women and Confusion." The box, which is now close to overflowing, contains more than a hundred articles about what it's like to be a woman in today's world.

In it, I have gathered a variety of opinions, overviews, underviews, surveys, studies, polls, diatribes and polemics on such women-related subjects as: work, love, sex, men, children, cosmetic surgery, dieting, education, adolescence, divorce, menopause, health, illness, hormones, role models, aging, beauty, assertiveness, money and anything else you can think of.

And, while I make it a practice to read each article before tossing it into the box, I had forgotten — until last Sunday, when I reread some of the material — just how wildly mixed the messages are that women receive from such articles.

Here, for example, are a few items selected at random from my "Women and Confusion" box:

Item: Working women who are wives and/or mothers are less apt to experience job-related, psychological stress than single, childless women.

Item: Working women who are wives and/or mothers are caught in a no-win juggling act that undermines both their role at work and their role at home.

Item: Women who remain single are less prone to depression than married women.

Item: Women who live in a family-setting suffer less anxiety and fewer depressive symptoms than single women.

Item: In marriages where husbands actually do a lot of housework and share family responsibilities, there is more — not less — conflict between spouses.

Item: Couples who share household duties are more satisfied in their relationships than those who don't.

Item: Men want women to be more assertive in sexual matters.

Item: Men still prefer women who are more submissive in sexual relationships.

Does all this confuse you as much as it does me?

So many messages. So many conflicting conclusions. What's a woman to believe?

A lot less than we read, in my opinion.

It was author Susan Faludi, of course, who nailed down in "Backlash: The Undeclared War Against American Women" the flimsiness of so many of the "scientific" statistics and studies claiming this or that theory about today's women. Remember all those statistics about women and marriage and terrorists? About women and depression and men?

Faludi scrupulously and relentlessly tracked them back to their sources and totally demolished the credibility of such studies.

But beyond the questionable studies and polls showing what women want — or don't want — lies the treacherous minefield of wildly fluctuating popular theories about what constitutes the proper role for today's woman.

In her book, "Erotic Wars: What Happened to the Sexual Revolution?" Lillian Rubin writes that women are placed increasingly in the position of having to make sense of an incredible number of mixed messages:

"Be an equal, but not wholly so. ... Be assertive, but ready to give way. Make money, but not too much. Commit to a career, but be ready to stay home with the children. Be sexually aggressive, but ..."

And when it comes to what's an "acceptable" role for women, writes Rubin, men are still calling the shots.

Well, maybe.

When I think about what's possible for women today, I always get bogged down at the point where work and family intersect. Even if such things as good day care, understanding employers and supportive husbands were universally guaranteed to working mothers, I'm not sure that women can ever fully avoid the "discontinuity" of a mother's life.

"I have never had a 'career,'" wrote Nobel Prize winner Alva Myrdal, an author and diplomat who began her professional life at 47, after her children were grown. "My path was more like a pleated ribbon where I, myself, nevertheless managed to insert one self-created activity after another."

Years later, Alva Myrdal's daughter would write that she learned from observing her mother that "the most profound curse on every woman's life ... is the uncertainty of her life plan, given the conflicting hopes and expectations she faces."

Every working woman with children knows what it means to be caught between conflicting hopes for yourself and the expectations of family.

Is it a dilemma that can be solved by equalizing the roles of men and women? By dividing up parenthood more equitably between mothers and fathers? Time, I guess, will tell.

As for me: My head says yes. But my heart says no.   ⊕

35

All About Eve

T here is a scene in the classic 1950 movie "All About Eve" when Bette Davis, playing the role of Margo Channing — a talented, wealthy, famous, but aging Broadway star — turns to a female friend and spits out her thoughts on what women need to be happy and whole:

(*Note to reader.* To get the full flavor of what follows, it's best to imagine Bette Davis wrapped in a mink coat, puffing furiously on her cigarette before making little circles in the air with the lit end, and, finally, releasing each word as if it were a grenade — with the pin pulled out. Sorry for the interruption; it seemed important. Now back to the dialogue.)

Miss Davis: *"In the final analysis, unless you can look up just before dinner or turn around in bed and he's there, you're not a woman. You're just something in a French provincial office."*

I estimate I've seen "All About Eve" a dozen times. And my reaction over the years to those particular lines is, in a way, like a map of where I've been and where I am. As a woman, that is, who married and had children in the 1960s. And got divorced in the 1970s.

Where I've been:

Growing up — in those years before adolescence opened a door to a wider vista — my parents' life together was what I knew of marriage, of relationships between men and women. It was a time when no one had heard of Betty Friedan or something called the Women's Liberation Movement.

And my mother's life reflected the philosophy expressed in "All About Eve": She was a woman who needed to look up at the end of the day and see my father. And, by the way, this is not a criticism; it's an observation made with love and, necessarily, in retrospect. My mother never worked outside of the house; her world revolved around her husband and children — as did the lives of most of my friends' mothers.

(I regret to this day that I never questioned my mother about this part of her life: Did she ever dream of having a career? Or regret that she didn't? It was only after her death, when I discovered some journals she kept — bits and pieces of writing she'd done which startled me with their promise — that I wondered: What would her life have been if it hadn't revolved so completely around a man?)

And back in those days — even though my friends and I were encouraged by our mothers to go on to college — the unspoken expectation was that we would meet a man and earn our "Mrs." before graduation.

And most of us did.

For some of us, it worked — the idea that women were defined by having a man — and for some of us it didn't. The latter group spent a lot of time reading the "Can This Marriage Be Saved?" column in *Ladies Home Journal.*

But you have to remember those were changing times; and not very many women — or men, for that matter — were able to fine-tune and balance the task of inhabiting a *whole* life; one which included careers as well as motherhood for women and, for men, more family involvement in addition to careers.

This was the time in my life when my women friends and I —

37

divorced or about to be divorced — would watch "All About Eve" and guffaw at the regressive, out-of-date sentiment expressed by Bette Davis.

Where I am:

(*Note to reader.* When someone says they know exactly where they are, often they're totally lost. Just a piece of cautionary advice about the following. Sorry about the interruption and thanks for your attention.)

So. Two weeks ago I watched "All About Eve" on television. Earlier in the evening, I'd had dinner with a woman friend and we'd talked about being single, about second acts in life, and about the wish to share a life with a significant other.

So here comes Bette Davis and I found myself hearing the lines about women, men and French provincial offices, and this time I didn't laugh. I also didn't cry. Which is to say I found myself thinking about how sometimes life does seem to go in a circle and that, to paraphrase T. S. Eliot, it's possible to find yourself back where you started and know the place for the first time.

Translation: I'm remembering — maybe for the first time — that a relationship can be a wonderful thing, as long as it has room enough and strength enough to support two full lives. It's a thought that makes a lot of doors swing open. ⊕

ALICE STEINBACH

A Matter Of Appearance

Quite a few people I know admit to experiencing a sense of shock when forced to confront a photograph of themselves. "My God," they'll say, smacking their forehead in surprise and cringing at the face in the picture, "is this what I really look like?"

The answer, usually, is: "Well, yes, this is what you look like. And, no, you do not bear a resemblance to Michelle Pfeiffer or Kevin Costner or anyone who appears in ads for Vogue *or* Esquire.*"*

Sorry about that.

Actually, the inability to reconcile the difference between what you look like and what you think you look like or want to look like seems to be an equal-opportunity experience. It afflicts both women and men; both young and old; both celebrity and non-celebrity.

It's a funny thing. After the teen years, appearance (read: good-looking or not good-looking) is supposed to matter only to those who are shallow and lack the ability to appreciate true, inner beauty. But in most of us, the wish to be physically attractive dies hard.

Once, a photographer was taking a picture of me that would be seen twice a week in the newspaper. He warned me I might be disappointed in the results. "Sometimes there's a problem when you columnists see the picture," he said. "It has to do with self-image."

Actually, I rather liked the way my photo turned out. It didn't look anything like me. It looked better.

Youth and Beauty

ot too long ago, a man I know — and like — said to me:
"I'll bet you must have been pretty when you were younger." Then he
paused, as though waiting for a reply.

Reply? What was I supposed to say — "Thank you very much"? But
it didn't matter because, before I could answer, the man moved on to
another subject. Politics or the weather or maybe it was baseball — I
really don't remember.

I don't remember because *I* had not moved on. I was still hearing the
words, "I'll bet you must have been pretty when you were younger." And
to tell the truth, my heart sank. At least a little.

But I was too busy at that moment to analyze my feelings. I did it
later, in front of my bathroom mirror.

Studying my face in the mirror, I wondered: What did his remark
mean and how upset should I be about it?

But instead of thinking about that, I found myself thinking about
this: It would never occur to me to assess whether this man, now in his
late 40s, looked better or worse when he was younger. Although when I

try to imagine it, I tend to think he's probably more attractive, not less attractive, now.

Then I found myself thinking about how a friend of mine, a beautiful woman of 42, recently plunked herself down at the lunch table and announced: "I've lost my looks. I looked in the mirror this morning and realized they were gone. Forever."

Then, in what was turning into a stream-of-consciousness, free-association experience, I thought suddenly of a question raised by another friend on the subject of youth and beauty. Or, more precisely, the passing of youth and beauty:

"When is a woman too old to flirt?" she asked. "I mean, I think that must be a sure sign of aging — when you don't flirt anymore for fear of seeming silly."

For some reason I thought of Marilyn Monroe, who, when she died in 1962 at age 36, was widely considered to be "washed up" as a sex symbol. Not only by Hollywood producers but, I have read, by herself. I have also read that near the end, when the always insecure movie star was suffering from paralyzing self-doubt, she would spend almost an entire day getting ready for a brief public appearance.

And that association brought me to Colette — who understood women as no other writer does — and of her observation that a woman's attempt to look good while suffering is a form of heroism. "The heroism of a doll," she wrote, "but heroism just the same."

But getting back to Marilyn Monroe: Thirty-six may have been old in 1962, but look, that was 30 years ago. Today is different. Isn't it? After all, we've got Jane Fonda, Raquel Welch, Sophia Loren and Gloria Steinem, all in their 50s and 60s now. And all glamorous.

Thinking of Gloria Steinem led me to think of another feminist, Simone de Beauvoir. Although she wrote of the need to free women from stultifying, preconceived ideas about age and beauty, she apparently was unable to follow her own advice.

"All her life, Simone de Beauvoir worried about growing old," writes her biographer, Deirdre Bair. "Indeed, many of her attitudes, such as thinking herself too old to be sexually active or attractive before she was even 40, might be laughable were they not so sad."

Which says, I guess, that being a feminist does not protect you from the hurts and losses that accompany the aging process. And that deep down it doesn't matter whether or not the losses have been foisted upon you by a male-dominated concept of beauty and desirability. The fact is: A loss is a loss is a loss.

And what a huge loss it must be to the woman who has staked everything on physical attractiveness and desirability when time drains that away. It seems unfair that the attractiveness of men — their sexual value, particularly — is derived not from their appearance, as with women, but from their achievements.

So I look in my bathroom mirror and wonder: How upset should I be that a man I know — and like — has said to me, "I'll bet you were pretty when you were younger"? But instead I find myself thinking about how there was a time, historically, when people had no mirrors and therefore had no idea what they looked like.

I can't imagine it: not knowing what you look like. But it occurs to me that if you weren't able to check out the aging process in the mirror, you'd just go through life always feeling like the same person — regardless of age.

But mirrors do exist. And so does the aging process. In fact, there's a word for the process that takes us from youth to old age. It's called: Life. ⊕

43

Fashion: Sense And Non-Sense

The sixty-something woman standing next to me at the gourmet carryout counter — the one ordering Caesar salad for two — was dressed in a twenty-something mode: sleek black tights, an oversized white shirt, and a tomato-red, hand-knit sweater jacket.

She was as slim as a teen-ager and as elegant as Audrey Hepburn, and the outfit suited her perfectly. The woman had a flair, no doubt about it. I noticed the stares — from envious to admiring — as women, both young and not-so-young, passed by.

And although I had never seen her before in my life, I recognized this striking woman instantly.

She was the grown-up version of the girl who haunted me all through school — from kindergarten to 12th grade. The girl who instinctively knew when pastel-colored angora sweaters were out and brown ski sweaters with little reindeer patterns all over the front were in; when brown penny loafers needed to be chucked out in favor of black Capezio slippers; when long, straight hair needed to be cut into a cropped, sexy style.

Yes, that woman standing there at the gourmet carryout counter was none other than Bunny Stubbs.

You, no doubt, also remember Bunny Stubbs. She had a different name, of course, but remember when you were in sixth grade? It was Bunny who showed up at the Ten Oaks swim party wearing her father's large, white button-down shirt knotted over her black bathing suit.

And remember in eighth grade when you went to Saturday matinees and sat two rows in front of those cute 10th grade boys? Well, it was Bunny who dreamed up the idea of wearing jodhpurs and riding boots with a white cashmere sweater to the festivities.

And wasn't Bunny the first girl in your class to wear navy blue with green?

Fashion, I'm convinced, is a Zen thing: It comes from within, is based on intuition, and often is an anti-rational act. Knowing, for instance, that you really can wear navy blue with green has always struck me as an incredible insight.

What I'm saying is that it's no good trying to be fashionable. Either you have a fashion sense or you don't. And if you don't — but refuse to admit you don't — then you run the considerable risk of becoming a "fashion victim."

I know a couple, for instance — both of them bright and talented attorneys — who refuse to confront the fact they are among the fashion-impaired. Instead of giving in and wearing what suits them best — simple, straight skirts and silk blouses in her case; tailored suits and Brooks Brothers shirts in his — they try every new trend that comes along.

The last time I had dinner with them, I was shocked to see their condition. The man was clearly in an advanced state of Ralph Lauren. His wife, whom I had a hard time distinguishing from the flowered chintz sofa, was obviously suffering from a severe Laura Ashley overdose.

I can say all this because I know what it's like to be someone who wants to be Bunny Stubbs, who has tried to be Bunny Stubbs, and who has failed miserably at being Bunny Stubbs.

I can say all this because — just when I thought I was getting over my wish to be one of the first to really understand why it's OK and not unprofessional to wear a short, black tulle skirt and long jacket to work — I find myself face-to-face with: "Bunny Stubbs — The Sequel."

Yes, here where I work, there's a woman who's so cool, looks so great, is so strikingly original in the way she wears clothes, that I've actually found myself backsliding. For instance, I found myself asking her about what kind of shoes go best with leggings.

Of course, that came after I asked her what leggings were and why would anyone want to wear the bottom half of a snowsuit.

Well, I didn't get what she was telling me, so the next time she wore her leggings to work, my colleague kindly walked me through the proper accessories for such an outfit.

I am now the proud possessor of such an outfit, but I haven't worn it. My wariness may be a result of the disastrous "Nancy Sinatra episode" in the '60s when I copied her white lips, white vinyl boots, doe eyes and miniskirt look and made the mistake of leaving the house looking like that.

By the way, do you have any idea what a "cat suit" is? I visualize it as a tailored suit with pointed ears and a tail. Well, whatever it is, I'll bet that, right now, even as I write these words, Bunny Stubbs is wearing one. ⊕

46

Charm School

T ry as I might, I can never remember whether it was my Aunt Claire or the late cosmetics queen Helena Rubinstein who made the following observation: "There are no ugly women, only lazy ones."

In the 1950s, such thinking was part of the feminine *Zeitgeist*. It accounted for, among other beauty aids, the push-up bra, the panty girdle and the invention of the home permanent. In my case, it also accounted for a gift certificate on my 17th birthday from Aunt Claire enrolling me in Miss Walters' Charm School.

It was kind of a last-ditch effort on Aunt Claire's part to turn me — her only niece — into a more glamorous (*read*: more marriageable) young woman. It might help to understand that Aunt Claire, married but childless, was the sophisticated, European-bred sister in my mother's family. Someone who lived year-round in a hotel and had two fur coats as well as a matched set of luggage — including a steamer trunk — which she always seemed to be packing. Or unpacking.

By the time Aunt Claire decided to take me under her wing and pass on her philosophy that feminine beauty and charm were acquired traits, not inborn ones, my personal best in the charm category resided in my popularity with other girls. And their parents. It was a trend which Aunt Claire disapproved of, pointing out that, should it continue, it would lead straight to Spinsterhood.

(And remember: All this happened B.C., which is to say, Before *Cosmopolitan* magazine and the Helen Gurley Brown philosophy that nobody — nobody! — has to remain a mouseburger all her life.)

Aunt Claire would deliver herself of such opinions late on Saturday afternoons while sipping a martini. Then she would quiz me on personal habits: *Why do you wear your hair like that? What do you plan to do about those freckles? Do you use a hand cream and wear gloves to bed at night?*

Aunt Claire's own hands and nails, of course, were always perfect: long, elegant fingers tipped with dark red lacquer and white half-moons; hands that were accustomed to holding the stems of martini glasses and wearing soft, crushed leather gloves. Once, she took me to her hairdresser, Mr. George, and asked him to "style" my hair. He styled it just like Aunt Claire's: a French twist with two looping waves over the forehead. Perfect for Aunt Claire; a disaster for me. I looked like a young Eleanor Roosevelt.

It was at about this point that Aunt Claire enrolled me in Miss Walters' Charm School.

Located in an elegant downtown building on upper Charles Street, Miss Walters' Charm School occupied the floor just above the Arthur Murray Dance Studios, and whenever the elevator stopped on the Arthur Murray floor, you would hear the sounds of cha-cha music. (Aunt Claire later tried to enroll me there, too, but that's another story.)

Charm School consisted of a number of rooms carpeted in dove gray and lined with floor-to-ceiling mirrors. ("Posture, girls, posture!" Who could forget with all those mirrors around?) One room had a dining table and appropriate settings of silver, china, serving dishes, etc.; everything the young hostess needed to give the correct dinner party.

Miss Walters, a former model, was a tall, handsome, slightly over-the-hill blonde who always — always — wore a hat. The rest of her wardrobe consisted of severely cut but elegant suits and high-heeled pumps, always in black, navy or brown. Colored shoes, we learned immediately, were a definite *non-non*. I don't even want to think what Miss Walters would have made of the idea of women in running shoes.

In charm school, we were taught how to sit, stand and walk; how to apply makeup ("Subtle, subtle, girls!"); how to find our best looks in hairstyles and wardrobe; how to read a menu in French; and, above all, how to be "charming." Unfortunately, I forget exactly how that last part went.

When I emerged six weeks later from Miss Walters' Charm School, I no longer looked like a young Eleanor Roosevelt. I looked like a middle-aged Eleanor Roosevelt.

Many years later, Aunt Claire and I sat together in her hotel room in Scotland — she lived in hotels until her death several years ago — and laughed about my short-lived experience as a Charm School graduate. Still, some things never change.

Like all inspired people, she remained, to the end, true to her goal: Trying to turn her little mouseburger into a filet mignon. She always did have expensive tastes.

One of the last things Aunt Claire ever said to me was this: *Have you ever thought of having your nails professionally manicured?*   ⊕

49

Losing It

I have to write this really fast because tomorrow I've got to show up at a friend's swimming pool.

In a swimsuit.

Which means I have only one day left to accomplish my goal of losing 10 pounds before appearing — in broad daylight — in clothing that resembles underwear.

The good news is I had the foresight to start my diet two weeks ago. The bad news is I still have 9-1/2 pounds to lose.

I'm not sure why it's taking so long. Perhaps a quick look at my diet notebook will offer some clues.

Day One: Weigh myself on bathroom scale. Numbers seem faint and far away. Difficult to see. Can't decide whether last two numbers are 30 or 80. Neither seems to make any sense but decide to go with 30.

Dress and go to supermarket to shop for food that is low cal, lite, no cholesterol, fat-free, etc., etc. Study label on can of Pork and Beans Xtra Lite. Print very small. Hard to read. Get out article that tells how to determine fat percentage in food.

It says: "If a serving has 256 calories and 4 grams of fat, multiply 4 by 9 to get 36 fat calories per serving. Divide the fat calories by total calories and multiply by 100 to get fat percentage."

Decide to take a pass on pork and beans and buy bottle of diet chocolate egg cream soda instead. Attractive young woman who's handing out sample cups of the soda assures me it's low in calories. Print on bottle too small to tell whether it's 28 calories or 280. Will take her word for it.

Load up cart with many varieties of frozen dinners that are lite, low cal, no cholesterol, fat-free, etc., etc.

Stop on way home for cappuccino but promise to spend ten extra minutes on treadmill. Maybe one day next week.

Or the week after.

Day Four: Am dismayed to read in newspaper that dieting has become politically incorrect. Decide that if I had not blown entire month's food budget on diet menu — lite food, it turns out, costs big $$$$ –— I could get behind this kind of political platform. Jot down a reminder in my "Things to Think About" journal: "Think about Lite Politics."

Decide to do some lite reading. Am halfway through "The 100 Best Chocolate Cake Recipes of All Time" when phone rings.

Friend on the other end asks if I know anything about the Swiss Sleeping Diet. Says she's heard you fly to a Swiss clinic where they keep you lightly sedated and dozing for two weeks, after which they wake you up and you're 15 pounds lighter. Says she heard all the big movie stars do it.

Get on scale. Numbers hard to read but think I see some movement in little arrow that points to numbers.

Mail arrives with announcement from niece that she's now the mother of an 8 pound, 3 ounce baby girl named Patricia Grace. Realize that's just 1 pound and 7 ounces less than I have to lose. Don't know why, but I find the calculation depressing.

Turn in early, at about 4 p.m., after a lite supper. That way I avoid

51

nighttime snacking. Wake up at 5:30 p.m. from a dream that house has turned into a gallon of Ben & Jerry's double, double, chocolate, chocolate ice cream. Lite, of course.

Get up and decide to go out for cappuccino. Promise to work it off on treadmill. Sometime soon.

Day Eight: Go to dinner party. Food theme seems to be related somehow to butter, cheese, and cream, etc., etc. After creamed chicken course and before coconut whipped cream pudding dessert, try to take my mind off food by feigning interest in what other people at party are saying:

"… and then I said, 'If you walk out that door without your sweater, don't blame me if you get pneumonia.. ' "

"… just sat down next to her without even asking if it was OK… "

"… long lines everywhere and there had to be more than 10 items in her cart. "

Make a mental note to write down in my "Highly Overrated Things" notebook that conversation among humans is not what it's cracked up to be.

Day 12: Go to supermarket again. Standing in front of meat counter, I cannot remember why I'm there. Then I realize it finally has happened: I am suffering from diet-induced butcher's block.

At home, get on scale. Spirits go way down. Little arrow pointer stuck at same place it was last week. Hard to read, but last two numbers are either 29 or 79.

Then read in newspaper about a new line of "user-friendly" swimsuits. Something called Slim Suit. Cleverly designed with an inner lining that works like a body girdle, the Slim Suit is guaranteed to make you look an inch thinner. Spirits soar.

On way to buy Slim Suit, decide to celebrate. Have a double cappuccino. Promise to work it off on treadmill. One day this year.

Or next. ⊕

Hair Problems

I am so tired I barely have the energy to write this. For the last three nights, I've been up, unable to sleep, just worried sick about two friends who were undergoing corrective cosmetic procedures over the weekend. I should be seeing them both any minute now, when they show up for work, and I don't mind telling you that I'm nervous as all heck.

I mean, the potential for disaster is great. What if they look so different I don't recognize them? *Excuse me, Miss. But you can't sit there. That desk is already taken by someone. Someone, I might add, who doesn't look like you.*

Of course, they could always look wonderful. But since I've had this procedure done myself — several times, in fact — I know how unlikely such an outcome is apt to be.

But, hey! Going into this deal, my friends knew the odds were against them. Both have had perms before.

Perm. As in permanent wave — the thing you do to your thin, straight hair after seeing Julia Roberts in "Pretty Woman."

In fact, Julia Roberts' name came up last Friday when my friends talked to me for hours about their hopes and dreams, their ambitions and goals in life. Perm-wise, that is.

"I'm going for the 'big hair' look," said my straight-haired Friend No. 1, who hasn't had a perm for several years but still meets people at parties who ask what happened to her old hair — the hair that was curly.

Friend No. 2 had a different look in mind: "I'm going for the 'exactly the way I look without a perm' look," she said. "My goal is to have a perm that doesn't look like a perm."

(*Note to the uninitiated:* a body perm is the scientific name for a perm that gives body — as opposed to curls — to your hair. The hypothesis is that hair with body is hair that will stand away from your head and look big instead of laying there, limp and lifeless like seaweed framing your face.)

But despite their different goals (one wants body, the other wants big, remember?) both women expressed a deep-seated fear regarding what they were about to do.

Friend No. 1: "I'm so nervous. Maybe I should do this just before I go on vacation to Portugal for two weeks. Just in case something terrible happens."

Me: "What are you afraid of?"

"That I'll look stupid and people will think I'm a fool."

Friend No. 2 surprised me by assuming a casual attitude toward the whole thing: "Usually I don't go out for three days after a perm," she said, "but I have plans to go out Sunday." Sensing she was hiding something, I used the reporter's oldest trick in the book. I remained silent. It worked. Suddenly the dam broke and all the latent perm anxiety stored up in her unconscious flooded out, like a stream-of-consciousness passage in a James Joyce novel:

I would rather go to the dentist than have a permanent ... If I call in sick on Monday, you'll know it's bad. If I call in sick Tuesday, send flowers. If you don't hear from me by Wednesday, it means — get to my house immediately to pull my head out of the oven. And be sure in the obituary it says I had glossy, dark hair alive with red highlights that drove men wild until the tragic visit to the hairdress-

er. And that I looked like Victoria Principal.

It was at this point that a Perm Support Group began to form around my desk, each woman revealing a perm combat horror story. It started to take on a kind of "Can You Top This" tone: *I had a perm so bad I had to get my hair entirely cut off my head ... I had a perm where they left the solution on so long it burned my hair into frizz ... I had a perm that turned my hair green ... I had a perm once ...*

Well, you get the idea.

As for me, I've paid my dues, *perm*anently speaking. If I had to pick my favorite personal horror story, it probably would be the episode that occurred when I was about 10 years old and an uncle had his girlfriend give me a home permanent.

Does the phrase "Bride of Frankenstein" conjure up a mental picture for you?

But, look. That's not going to happen to my two friends. Perms have come a long way since then. And besides, if things should go bad — and don't get me wrong, I'm not saying they will go bad — there are always haircuts. Or hats.

And if that doesn't work: Venice, anyone?   ⊕

Fashion: More Sense and Non-Sense

Even after it has been carefully explained to me by one of my most stylish friends, I still don't understand why I can't wear a black-leather biker jacket with a tweed skirt and brown leather walking shoes.

"I don't get it," I tell her. "I saw *Vogue* editor Anna Wintour on TV this morning and she said black is in. She said leather is in. And she said biker jackets are in. So where did I go wrong?"

"By not accessorizing your jacket with a silver catsuit and panther-print platform pumps," my friend shot back in that annoying, know-it-all tone of voice used by people who, annoyingly, know it all.

Such are the realities of life, I guess. That one kind of person approaches the new fall fashion season with a sense of certainty and ongoing personal growth, while another sort of person approaches it cautiously.

Or to put it another way: Some people get their first glance of the "Terminatrice" look (think Linda Hamilton in a black T-shirt with cutoff sleeves, black chino pants, black boots) and immediately think, "Why not?"

Others get a gander at such an outfit and think, "Huh?"

Still others — myself included — greet each fashion change in much the same way that Dorothy Parker met all new events in life: by wearily and warily asking the rhetorical question, "What fresh hell is this?"

It is a question that was never far from my mind while leafing through a recent fashion magazine. How, I wondered, could I possibly incorporate into my existing wardrobe such items as a jacket flared at the hem to resemble the line of a hula hoop? Or thigh-high, patent leather boots with Lucite heels? Or a see-through, silver mesh blouse and beaded biker shorts?

(In all fairness, I should point out that few women I know could successfully carry off that last look — not even Martha Stewart, a woman who seems to be in complete control of the universe as we know it.)

In a scholarly paper I hope to write someday — one which attempts to pinpoint the influences in an individual's life which shape her, or his, fashion persona — I plan to use my own life to illustrate my hypothesis. The following is a rough outline of the paper which I have titled simply: "Seven People Who Made Me What I Am Today — Fashionwise."

1. Eileen down the street: As early as the age of two, I recognized that my friend Eileen wore her sunsuits with a flair unachieved by anyone else in the sandbox. Very influential.

2. Miss Ford, my kindergarten teacher: A former WAC, she opened up the unlimited possibilities of khaki as a color. Pretty influential.

3. The O'Brien twins, Maureen and Mary, in the sixth grade: A classic and important scientific lesson in how genetics do not the fashion persona make. Although identical twins, Maureen was a fashion winner — gold circle pin, cashmere sweater, pleated skirt — and Mary a fashion disaster — brown shoes with navy socks, unmatched barrettes, tartan skirt with striped blouse. Darn influential.

4. My paternal Aunt Claire: A woman who knew how to wear a fur coat with a corsage of violets. Huge but mostly symbolic fashion influence since I don't wear a fur coat and seldom get corsages.

5. Miss Lillian, a saleswoman in Hutzler's Better Hats Department:

"You should never wear purple," Miss Lillian told me once when I was about 12 and tagging along with my mother on a shopping trip. "It will make your skin look blue." Very influential, particularly when applied in concert with the khaki-color tips from Miss Ford, my kindergarten teacher.

6. LaRue Martin, a cheerleader in my junior high school: From LaRue, who was two grades ahead of me, I learned the art of wearing the proper-sized sweater. Less, I learned, is more. Her influence lives on.

7. Yves Saint Laurent, the fashion designer: Interviewed him in 1985 and found his advice on fashion most helpful. "The best possible look," he said, "is a simple black blouse worn with a simple black skirt." At least I think that's what he said. Since he was speaking in French — not my first language — and I was wearing a black blouse and black skirt, I may have misunderstood. Still, he probably ties with the O'Brien twins (Maureen and Mary, remember?) for most influential.

I'm also planning to do a paper devoted to the analysis of my recurring fashion nightmare. The one in which my photo is featured in the *National Enquirer* under the headline: "Worst Dressed Celebrities at the Academy Awards." Featured along with me are Cher, Heather Locklear and, oh yes, the O'Brien twins. ⊕

ALICE STEINBACH

Raising Children

Let's begin with that old, familiar line from Charles Dickens: "It was the best of times, it was the worst of times." As far as I'm concerned, that about sums up what it's like to raise children.

More than any other endeavor in life, parenting forces us to confront the deepest and widest range of emotions possible. Love, fear, joy, worry, anger, hopes and dashed hopes: only in the act of raising a child do we tap into the deepest reserves of such feelings. And only in the service of raising a child do we summon up an ability to love far beyond anything we imagined.

In raising my children, I have laughed, wept, worried, been happy beyond belief and sad past all accounting, yelled, given up, cheered, been proud, been disappointed (mostly in myself), thrown things, been selfish and unselfish, been comforting and comforted, and felt overworked and underappreciated — sometimes all in the same day.

But somewhere along the way, in the middle of all the loving and shouting, the worrying and hoping, I learned something about myself that I would never have known in a life without children: that I am capable of loving two other human beings, my sons, unconditionally.

The way I see it, life doesn't get much better — or at times much worse — than that.

Mother's Day

The lilacs bloomed last week, reminding me it was time to send
Mother's Day cards to my sons.

I guess it's more accurate to describe them as Mother's Day letters,
these scribbled notes I send to my sons each year at this time.

It's not traditional, I know. On Mother's Day, mothers are supposed
to receive cards from their children, not send them.

But for some reason, I've always thought of Mother's Day not as a
time to expect some kind of special treatment from the sons, but as a
time to let them know how profoundly grateful I am for their existence.
And how I can't imagine life without them.

Of course, you have to be careful about writing down this kind of
stuff. You don't want to embarrass your kids. And you don't want to
embarrass yourself.

So you don't really tell them of your profound gratitude and that
you can't imagine life without them. You write instead of how wonderful
the Christmas visit was and how pleased you are at the way their lives are
going and how you can't wait to see them again in the summer.

You write such things to your sons and hope they read between the lines. And over the lines. And under the lines.

But sometimes on a spring day such as this — a day when the white dogwoods and purple lilacs explode with color outside the kitchen window — I find myself composing a letter in my head.

It's a letter to my sons that will never be written. But if it were, it would go something like this:

Not so many years ago, I stood and watched the two of you playing from this window. And if I close my eyes now, I see you still: Two boys — one dark-haired, the other fair — intent on wringing out every minute of the light before darkness sent you indoors.

One of you was always doing something with a ball: bouncing it off steps or shooting hoops or throwing it at someone's bat.

And one of you was always looking up at the sky, consulting your charts and maps and getting your telescope ready for the starry night watch that fascinated you.

Do you remember the long walks you took with your grandmother when you were little? I do.

What I remember best is how each of you always presented me with a small bunch of wildflowers when you came home: delicate Queen Anne's lace and blue cornflowers and occasionally a Mexican rose that had forced its way through the sidewalk cracks.

It's funny, but I always loved the fact that the two of you were, and are, so very different in the way you see the world.

One so trusting, the other so questioning. One so neat, the other not so neat. One who loved the camaraderie of team sports, of baseball and basketball. And one who sought out the solitary challenges of mountain climbing and skiing.

But you shared, and still share, a common thread that weaves in and out of whatever it is we call the essence of a person: a wonderfully funny — and surprisingly comforting — sense of humor.

Another thing: I'll never forget and always will treasure the memory of how kind you both were to your grandmother — my mother — when she was dying.

You were teen-age boys at the time with an agenda that included all the tur-

moil that accompanies adolescence. And yet you were there when it counted for your grandmother.

I like to think — no, actually I know it to be true — that because of you, her death was not a lonely one.

One of you once asked me why life was so hard sometimes and so easy at others. I didn't know the answer then, and I don't know it now.

But I have watched each of you live through both hard and easy times. And although it was often a mighty struggle to get through the hard times, you got through them. Without compromising your essential decency.

From you I have learned many things, the most important of which is: It is possible to love another human being without placing conditions on the relationship.

I've heard that in China there is a saying, "May you live in interesting times." I've never been sure whether it's meant as a curse or a benediction for a good life.

But my experience as a mother leads me to believe that if you really want to wish a person well, you might say: "May you live with interesting people." As I have with you.

Of course, this is not the letter I wrote to my sons. Instead, I scribbled a few lines about home and the cats and how I can't wait to see the sons again.

But this time I also placed a sprig of lilac inside each envelope.

And sometime today, with great pleasure, I will imagine my faraway sons opening the envelopes. And I will imagine their surprise as the scent of lilac jumps out, like a genie from a bottle, to remind them of home.

Of home and, I hope, of me. ⊕

Thanksgiving at the Holiday Inn

The son living in Japan called a few nights ago. "How long does it take to roast a 12-pound turkey and how do you make gravy?" he wanted to know.

That was the easy question.

The difficult question followed: "When do you think we'll all be together again on Thanksgiving for dinner?" He sounded wistful. Maybe even a little homesick.

It has been three years since the whole family gathered around one Thanksgiving table. Which, in my view, is exactly three years too many.

But as children grow up and the river of family separates into tributaries, each flowing in its own direction, it gets harder and harder to assemble everyone in the same place at the same time.

The son in Japan will celebrate Thanksgiving this year with a group of about 50 American and Japanese friends. You might say it's becoming a tradition: They buy two 12-pound turkeys — at a cost of $240 — and gather on the Saturday after Thanksgiving.

Although this means each person only gets one small serving of turkey, the son says it's definitely worthwhile. "Being away from home on Thanksgiving," he said, "is just as bad as not being there on Christmas."

The other son will be spending his day in a physics lab in Colorado, trying to catch up on work toward his graduate degree. I've sent him a pecan pie, his favorite, and some homemade cranberry jelly. But knowing him, the odds are he won't even remember it's Thanksgiving.

Until I call to remind him.

When they were growing up, my sons always wanted to have Thanksgiving dinner at home. And they always wanted exactly the same menu. No fancy stuffings or strange cranberry sauce or any pie other than pecan.

And usually that's exactly how the day went.

Except for the year my two sons and I found ourselves — for difficult reasons that no longer matter — eating Thanksgiving dinner at a Holiday Inn, far away from family and friends.

At the time, the older son was nine; the younger, six. Neither was thrilled to find himself in a strange restaurant on what had always been a family day at home.

And I was as unhappy about it as they were.

It was a day in which we were all just killing time. And getting on one another's nerves.

We'd spent the early afternoon seeing a movie called "Bedknobs and Broomsticks." It starred Angela Lansbury and, as I recall, had something to do with witchcraft and Nazis and a flying bed. We all hated it. Which was the only thing the three of us had agreed on the whole day.

Thanksgiving dinner, which took place in a revolving restaurant on the top floor of the Holiday Inn, was a disaster.

First of all, one of my sons claimed to be motion sick and the other said he couldn't eat at that altitude because he was afraid of heights. This is the same son, incidentally, who now spends much of his free time climbing mountains and scaling rocks.

But, of course, our unhappiness had nothing to do with the Holiday Inn or motion or heights. We were all just angry — and afraid, too.

65

Angry that things were not exactly what they had been and afraid they might never be that way again. So we did what all normal families do: We tried to cope by annoying each other. That, at least, was familiar.

As I remember it, most of our conversation at that Thanksgiving dinner revolved around what was worse: the turkey, the stuffing, the sweet potatoes, the gravy, the pumpkin pie, or the water that didn't taste like the water back home.

Which, of course, is where we all wanted to be.

For years I thought of that Thanksgiving as the worst I'd ever spent. In fact, it became a family joke: "Better do what Mom says or she'll make us have Thanksgiving dinner at the Holiday Inn again."

But lately I've come to realize that I was wrong.

Now I understand that because my sons and I were together that Thanksgiving, we *were* at home. And now I look back and see the day as a good example of what makes a family a family: the ability to express anger and frustration toward one another without fear of losing one another's love.

Now, I look almost with longing at that "worst" Thanksgiving I ever spent. I guess I've finally learned the lesson we all come to understand slowly: That we don't know how good a time we're having until it's part of the past. ⊕

Philosophers

So here we are, well into the second week of 1992, and here's my question to you: Is it too late for me to make a New Year's resolution?

No? Well, then, here it is: I resolve to never, ever give advice to any-one again for as long as I live. I further resolve to never break this rule no matter how pathetically someone begs or pleads for my advice.

There. I feel better already. In fact, I feel so good that my advice to you — oops, I mean, my suggestion to you — is to consider making the same resolution.

It's been building for a long time, this idea of removing myself from the advice business. But over the holidays it became clear that I could no longer put it off. Everyone I knew seemed to be in need of some bit of advice or another.

The problem with giving advice, of course, is that no one really wants to hear it, much less take it:

Son: "Mom, should I get my hair cut really short or leave it the way it is?"

Me (cautiously): "Well, I think really short hair would look great on you."

Son: "I knew it. I knew my hair looked awful this way."

Next case.

Friend who is thinking about changing careers: "So what do you think? Is it a mistake for me to make the move?"

Me (cautiously): "I think you'd really enjoy the work and do it well."

Friend: "In other words, you think I've been in the wrong field all along."

And so it went during the holidays. A small but steady stream of people asking for and then rejecting my advice. Which led me to this conclusion: When people ask for your advice, it's a trap. Avoid it. That's my advice — suggestion — to you.

And don't bother to write and tell me the fault lies in the way I dispense my advice. Over the years, I have paid my dues. Advice-wise, that is. As a parent, I left no avenue unexplored in seeking productive ways to dispense advice to my children.

When they were young, for example, I came up with the idea of disguising the advice in a parable or allegory.

Son: "Mom, why do all the other kids in fourth grade have good ideas for their science class diorama but I don't? What should I do?"

Me: "Son, I want to tell you a little story about Albert Einstein. Someone once asked this man — who was responsible for so many great discoveries — where he got all his ideas. 'The truth is,' he replied, 'I've only had one or two good ideas in my lifetime.'"

Son: "So you're saying that Einstein is smarter then me."

Not long after this exchange, I switched to the "fortune cookie" approach to advice-giving.

"Turn your stumbling blocks into stepping stones," I said when asked for advice on how to make the baseball team.

"Strong people are made by opposition — like kites that go up against the wind," I advised in the face of an algebra catastrophe.

As the kids moved into adolescence, I gave advice through the use of famous-people quotes.

When, for instance, advice was solicited on how to correct a slumping social life, I quoted Yogi Berra, who advised his slumping batters: "Swing at the strikes."

This method worked well until the kids reached high school and discovered "Bartlett's Book of Quotations." There followed a pretty bad spell as they decided to fight fire with fire.

"Opportunity is missed by most people because it is dressed in overalls and looks like work," I advised, quoting Thomas Edison.

"Work is the curse of the drinking classes," they countered, quoting Oscar Wilde.

Maybe it's my imagination, but when I was growing up, kids seemed to listen to what adults told them. My Aunt Claire's advice, for instance, to "always wear clean underwear in case you're hit by a car and have to go to the hospital" has never left me.

But that was then and this is now. And, as I said, I've given up the advice thing. There will be lapses, I'm sure. Why, just a few minutes ago, a colleague asked my advice on finding a street in the city that is unfamiliar to him. Forgetting that I don't give advice anymore, I quoted Yogi Berra: "You've got to be very careful if you don't know where you are going, because you might not get there."

By the way, since I'm no longer in the advice business, I'd like to make a gift of a piece of advice I've been saving up to use. It's from Ronald Reagan, who in 1976 advised environmentalists on the folly of their ways by saying, "Once you've seen one redwood, you've seen them all."

Feel free to use this advice in any way you see fit. ⊕

The World on a String

Generally speaking, the four things one hopes for most when staggering out of bed to face a new day are:

1. That you will not be greeted by a raging ice storm.
2. That you will not be faced with a bad hair day.
3. That your boss will not decide that today is the day to do your job evaluation.
4. That it's Friday. Or better yet, Saturday.

What one hopes for in the routine of everyday life, I have found, usually consists of such mundane wishes as these. After the age of 21 or thereabouts, one does not rise up from bed hoping for the world on a string.

A nice, uncomplicated commute to work, yes. A supper hour uninterrupted by phone solicitations, yes. But the world on a string? No. In fact, no thanks. I've always been a person who enjoys hoping on a small scale.

Small hopes, I've observed, are a lot like dogs: They tend to come when they're called.

Big hopes, on the other hand, are more like cats: you can call them all you want, but if they don't want to come, forget it.

There is, however, one exception to my small hope-big hope philosophy. It has to do with my sons.

When it comes to one's children, you want them to have big hopes. Of course you don't tell them this. Directly, that is. But, in subtle and not so subtle ways, parents are always telling their children to aim high in life.

That's the easy part. Aiming high. The hard part is having your hopes dashed when you miss your target. And the bigger the dashed hope, the bigger the disappointment. Helping a child to get past the disappointment and move on is one of the most important tasks facing a parent.

And, unfortunately, one of the most frequent.

But occasionally in the life of a parent, something wonderful happens. The phone rings, for instance, and suddenly hope — the thing with feathers that perches in the soul — flies out. It's in your son's voice, crackling across the telephone wires.

"I passed," my twenty-something son says, his voice filled with happiness and disbelief at having gotten past a major hurdle in his academic life. It was hard for him to accept that what he had so hoped for actually happened.

Hard for me to accept it too. Over the last several months, I had invested a lot of my hope capital in this son's account. But that's what parents do as their children move into their adulthood: They transfer into their children's accounts a lot of their own hopes and dreams.

"Happiness makes up in height," Robert Frost wrote, "what it lacks in length." He must have had the parent-child relationship in mind. When it comes to children, every parent knows that happiness has a short shelf life.

On the other hand, there seems to be no statute of limitations when it comes to worrying about a child. "When is it over?" I wonder. When does this intense identification with a child's hopes and disappointments end? The answer is: never.

The night of the phone call from my son, I wandered into his old room. It's still pretty much the way he left it, a teen-ager's shrine to his passion for skiing and climbing.

Such bright, happy reminders of a child's life. It made me think of something a Japanese poet wrote more than a thousand years ago about her wish to see her infant child grow into adulthood.

"I wish I could live long enough to see him soar high above the clouds," she wrote, "when his cloak of crane feathers has grown out with the years."

And for a moment I did see him, my son, soaring. And it didn't sadden me that in a sense he was soaring away from me. Like a string to a kite, I felt the tug of connection. ⊕

Lost and Found

This is how it begins: One night in early September, while watching TV, you decide to pop some corn. So you go into your kitchen to dig out the old popcorn machine, but it's nowhere to be found.

Then, a week or so later, you feel a chill in the air and decide it's time to get out the portable space heater. But after an hour or two of searching, you turn up nothing. Nada. Zilch. Zero.

The pace begins to quicken.

Over the next fortnight, you search for, and fail to find, such items as your hair dryer, Mr. Coffee machine, electric fan, teakettle, kitchen shears, assorted luggage, extra-large bath towels, hair mousse, Chinese wok, sewing kit, desk lamp, portable phone, electric blanket, transistor radio and electric blender.

As the mystery deepens — and the list of missing items grows — all kinds of scenarios run through your head. A cat burglar. Early senility. A friend who borrowed your luggage. A blanket deposited at the cleaners. The phone left at the beach.

Then, before you know it, it's the middle of October — the time when parents of college freshmen traditionally visit their kids on campus — and suddenly the Mystery of the Missing Household Items is solved: They are all residing in a room on a distant college campus — the one occupied by your college-age son or daughter.

Why is it, I wonder, that nobody warns parents that when your kids go away to college, so do all your small household appliances?

And why is it that none of the child experts — not even Dr. T. Berry Brazelton — sees fit to include this developmental phase in their books on raising children:

"At approximately the age of 18, the average, college-bound teenager goes through a period of relocating household appliances. A general rule of thumb is that after each visit home, the student takes at least four additional appliances and/or household items back to college."

My own first encounter with this developmental phenomenon occurred while walking across a campus on freshmen parents' weekend. From a distance, I spotted my son. Recognized him, in fact, by the sweater he was wearing — an intricately patterned ski sweater I purchased for him in Norway.

However, upon closer inspection, I confirmed that while it was, indeed, the aforementioned sweater, it was not my son.

"He lent it to me," said the young man who was not my son. He then directed me to my son's dormitory.

And what a pleasant surprise it was, upon arriving at the entry to my son's room, to be greeted by an old familiar friend — the "Welcome" mat that had disappeared from my very own front door just a month before.

Inside, I was made to feel equally at home. There, reclining among the batik-covered pillows from my den, I sipped a pineapple frappe from my blender and marveled at how many wonderful patterns could be formed just by stacking up assorted pieces of my luggage in an interesting way.

And the climate control in the room was excellent. My space heater going full blast in the bathroom produced, I thought, just the right temperature, even on a day when it was 85 degrees outside. Another plus about the bathroom was I got to use my own towels again — the monogrammed ones that had been given to me as a wedding gift.

I also enjoyed seeing my white, pearlized wastebasket and matching soap dish again. I'd forgotten how attractive they were.

To my surprise, I felt equally at home in the room across the hall. Invited there by my son's friend, I noted how attractive my desk lamp looked sitting next to my portable phone. And what good reception my radio got, even up here in the hills of the Berkshires.

From there, it was a movable feast over to a room occupied by another of my son's friends. The popcorn made in my popper never tasted better and I must say that my old patchwork quilt looked mighty good thrown across the back of his friend's futon.

In fact, I was so impressed with this recycling of household goods that I scarcely minded at Thanksgiving when the sleds disappeared from the garage. Or the disappearance after Christmas break of an Edward Hopper poster, a small side table, and a bedside reading lamp.

I minded even less at spring break when a number of sheets, pillowcases and pillows — along with a small desk chair — vanished. Actually, the house was beginning to look more spacious. Less cluttered, somehow.

What I did mind, however, was that awful day at the end of the school year when the son arrived home with a U-Haul trailer. I think you know what was inside. ⊕

Letters from Camp

Good advice, I have found, often turns up in the strangest places.

Recently, for example, I found the following piece of good advice in an old suitcase:

"Hooray! This is the fourth day I've been here at camp and I finally got my trunk today. At first it was awful because I only had what was in my dufflebag. But then it turned out I didn't need as much of that stuff as I thought I needed."

This wise observation — and who among us has not learned the hard way that we don't need a lot of the stuff we think we need — comes not from Thoreau but from Camp Deerwood, circa 1979.

Or, to be more precise: from a letter found along with dozens of others that record the thoughts of a son while away at summer camp. Hidden away in the suitcase for several years, the letters — along with those of his brother — turned up during a housecleaning binge.

But first, a word of caution: Do not — I repeat, do not — ever sit down to read letters written from camp if you are not prepared to spend most of the afternoon careening back and forth between laughter and tears, between happiness and sadness.

Actually, those feelings did not surprise me. What did surprise me was this: The feeling of how much I had missed in reading these letters the first time around. Of course, back then I was looking for signs that the sons were doing OK at camp — that they were physically healthy and emotionally happy.

But now, from this distance, the nearsightedness of parental vision has given way to a clearer view. And what leaps out at me from these Popsicle-stained letters is how much good advice lies in the unself-conscious observations of kids.

"Things are pretty good," wrote one of the sons from a camp in New Hampshire. "Swimming class started today. I am taking 'Survival' which is so hard because you have to swim in your clothes with your hands and feet tied. That comes later on though. So I will wait to worry about it then."

Meanwhile, his brother was writing home of a rather rocky start at his camp in North Carolina:

"The 4:50 plane did not leave until 6:35 because of brake trouble. Then due to an electrical storm, our plane was rerouted to Kinston so we arrived at camp really late. This morning it's already 90 degrees and raining hard. But that will give me a chance to work really hard in ceramics class on the striped whale I'm going to make."

(*Note to reader:* I still have the striped whale. And, in my opinion, it was worth the rain delay.)

Moving on to another letter, I see this bit of advice folded into a report from New Hampshire:

"We hiked 2.4 miles up a steep, tree-lined trail and then we broke above the timberline. It was spectacular! All the trees get gnarled until only lichen grows on the rocks. It's funny what looks beautiful to you when you look at things differently."

Of course, reading this letter reminds me that its writer always had an eye for spotting a different kind of beauty. Particularly in nature. And, I might add, in his choice of ties.

77

Happiness is the subject of a letter from a camp in West Virginia. Its young author wrote:

"Today we saw the 'Muppet Movie.' It was about Kermit who followed his dream to go to Hollywood. But on the way, a man named Doc Hopper wants Kermit to do a commercial for his company, selling frog legs. He even threatens Kermit. But Kermit sticks up for his dream. And because of that, he is one happy frog at the end."

And speaking of ends, I am particularly struck by the insight built into this observation:

"Yesterday we had a big campfire to celebrate the last Sunday of camp. Actually, we always have a campfire on Sundays, but this one was special. You know, the way the last time you do anything always seems special."

Time was also on the mind of the other son in the following letter.

"I think today is the 12th of August," he writes. "But I'm not sure. It's not like regular time down here. You don't think if it's a school day or the weekend. Because when you don't have to be somewhere on time, it doesn't matter very much."

After reading this, I drifted upstairs into a son's old bedroom. Not much has changed since he left: The ski posters still line the walls; the astronomy books remain stacked on his desk. But in the afternoon light, the room suddenly looked beautiful to me.

Funny, isn't it, what looks beautiful to you when you look at things differently?   ⊕

The Land of Adolescence

A dolescence, I have often observed, is like a foreign country. **79**
They do things differently there.

In the Land of Adolescence, for instance, customs quite distinct from those of adults are routinely adhered to by teen-agers. Among the more common manifestations of this foreign culture would be:

• Never beginning one's nightly social life before 11 p.m. Or later.

• Always scheduling one's time in the bathroom shower at a time when the bathroom shower is already in use.

• The routine ingestion of large quantities of food — usually some foodstuff along the lines of three bowls of Cocoa Puffs or half a chocolate cake — just before dinner.

• An intense preoccupation with hair mousse products and acne preparations.

• A style of dress usually involving clothing that is ripped and/or has holes in it.

• A concept of housekeeping that equates cleaning one's room with the gathering together of all loose items, which are then thrown into a closet.

• The round-the-clock playing of loud music featuring persons emitting strange, unintelligible sounds.

Question: Who was it who said that cute teen-agers exist only on television and never in your own house?

Which bring us to that most compelling of adolescent customs — the Morse Code used by teen-agers to communicate with one another. In the Land of Adolescence, it is the solemn duty of each of its citizens to learn a new language: Teenspeak.

Here, for instance, is a conversation between two teen-age girls I recently overheard at the mall.

Girl No. 1: "He's, like, really cool. OK? I mean, not, like, gross like his friends. I mean, I go, 'Let's go shop at the mall,' and he, like, goes, 'Cool.' So, like, I say, 'OK.' And it's, like, we both go, 'Cool,' at the same time."

Girl No. 2: "Cool. That's really, like, cool."

Of course, Teenspeak changes from generation to generation. One generation's "Dig you later" is another's "Hang loose, man."

But it is an ongoing phenomenon. In fact, linguists are studying Teenspeak and have come up with some interesting theories.

One Swedish linguist, for instance, believes that Teenspeak — and I am not making this up — is the spoken equivalent of the stream-of-consciousness technique used by some of our greatest writers. I mean, like, writers, you know, like James Joyce and Virginia Woolf.

Which, like, if it's true is, like, totally awesome. OK?

Still, there's another side to adolescence, one we often overlook: the idealism that burns beneath the surface. Indeed, in the span of a person's life, the teen years may represent the peak of idealism. It's an unlikely combination, this co-mingling in teens of self-obsession and altruism. But it exists.

I was reminded of it in a particularly vivid way recently on yet another trip to the mall.

After a spectacularly unsuccessful shopping trip — one spent trying to locate a bathing suit I was willing to wear outside my bedroom — I returned to find that my car had a flat tire. I kicked myself for not taking the time to do what I was always promising to do: take the course in car maintenance offered at a local college.

So I'm standing there, looking at my flat tire, when this beat-up Toyota pulls up next to me. Out jumps this teen-age boy who, to be blunt about it, looked as though he might be on his way to or from a reform school. If such a thing even exists anymore.

"Need some help?" he asked.

"You better believe it," I answered.

We talked as he changed my tire. A farmer's son from Georgia, he was up here visiting some relatives before taking off for California. He loved animals, he told me, and hoped to find some kind of job with the U.S. Park Service or maybe a zoo. I asked him if he ever thought about becoming a veterinarian. He said no, he wasn't smart enough. And besides, he didn't think he could ever bring himself to cut open an animal.

It's hard to describe the sweetness I felt coming out of this young man. Both in the way he helped me — a stranger — out of a jam and in the way he talked about the future. He was full of optimism and hope about life and what he could give and get back from that life.

"Now you take care," he said, as he sent me on my way. Through my rear view mirror, I saw him waving until I turned the corner.

Driving home, I thought about him, about the way he volunteered to help without being asked, and about how he refused to take money for it. And I wondered why we don't tap into this altruistic part of teen-agers more often.

And it made me remember my teen years too. Of how I dreamed of being a doctor who would discover some miracle cure. Or, if not that, then a tap dancer with the Rockettes. ⊕

81

Parents Are Forever

Once, a long time ago — for about a day — I tried to be the Perfect Mother: I listened intently to everything my children said, I baked cookies for them, I played Monopoly with them, I intervened in their fights politely, and I remained — no matter what disaster arose — unshakably, almost eerily, patient.

But I quickly found out two things about being the Perfect Mother. First, there is no such thing. And second, even if there were, no one — not even June Cleaver — could live up to such expectations.

Of course, it was a silly premise from the start — the idea that maternal perfection consists of paying constant and profound attention to your children. But I was young and green at the time, an inexperienced apprentice when it came to the job of mothering.

Most of what I knew about parenting I had learned from reading psychological how-to books on child rearing. And the point that had leaped out at me in book after book was: When it comes to raising healthy children, there are hundreds of ways in which it is possible to screw up completely.

But happily for me, my children were not as inexperienced at being children as I was at being a parent.

Don't ask my why, but kids seem to be born knowing how to be kids. You won't find them racing out to buy books on how to be a successful child or ways to deal with the many stages parents go through.

And children don't feel the kind of guilt about what they're doing to their parents that parents feel about what they're doing to their children. That little albatross comes later, when they have their own kids and have to figure out how to be a parent.

I thought about all of this recently — about the roles of parents and children and how they change over the years — when my now twenty-something sons returned home for a three-week stay. I looked forward to sharing a house with them again and the kind of contact that can happen only through the routines of daily life. And I wanted the satisfaction of observing these newly minted adults emerging from the children who were so familiar to me.

But as any parent who's been in this position can tell you, such a visit is not without its perils.

In fact, the pattern that accompanies the return of grown-but-not-yet-permanently-settled children to a parent's house is somewhat predictable: It resembles a roller-coaster ride.

First, there is a brief period of extreme harmony produced by an unnatural politeness on the part of all parties.

Next comes a period of disharmony produced by the surfacing of old, unsettled grievances. Falling apart at this point are both sides' great expectations that all the old parent–child roles will be replaced with new ones.

Finally — if you have the courage for it — the point arrives at which it's time for both sides to sit down, settle some old scores, and negotiate a different contract.

Of course, this is easier said than done. For one thing, it means listening to some criticisms you'd rather not face. The funny thing is, once all the old grievances are put on the table, it's sometimes possible to take a step closer to a more balanced relationship.

And that leads to seeing each other in fresh ways.

So what was I able to see from this new and still tentative position?

For one thing, I think I saw the outlines of a relationship based on honesty. Even when it's painful.

And I saw two people I liked. Decent people who are capable of deep feelings. And shallow feelings as well.

And I think I saw the emerging shape of a relationship based on this philosophical premise: Get over it. Which is to say, there seems to be an unspoken agreement to dump whatever negative baggage remains from the past and move on.

Still, it seems parenting ain't over till it's over. Which may turn out to be never.

I remember how my own mother, up to her very last breath, worried about what would happen to me — a grown woman with almost grown children — after her death.

Still, because the future is one of those invisible realities in which I believe, I'm looking forward to the exciting unfolding of these two people whom I know so well.

I hope I can change with them.

Of course, I'd like it a lot if some things didn't change.

For instance, I'd really be happy if the one son never got too old or too sophisticated to plant a kiss on the top of the cat's head, as he did just before he left last week.

And I'd be thrilled if the other son kept on planting a few tulip bulbs in the garden we created together when he was a teen-ager, as he did on his recent trip home.

In the world of parents like me, little things still mean a lot. ⊕

ALICE STEINBACH

The
Solo Life

When I was in Mrs. Hall's fourth-grade class, I got 22 valentines. By the age of 17, I'd already "gone steady" with three boys. At 21, I'd had two serious marriage proposals. The year I turned 22, I happily got married. And, a couple of decades later, I got divorced. That was followed by a wild and exciting period of playing the field, falling in love at least twice, becoming engaged once more, breaking off the engagement and, finally, settling down to the task of learning how to enjoy life with or without a partner.

Living, I have come to believe, is a work-in-progress. And so is being single. The modern complexities of single life have found their way into many television shows and movies. Indeed, there's a sitcom that embraces every kind of singlehood imaginable: the divorced single woman, the divorced single man, the single mother, the single father, and the older or younger single friends, both male and female, who live together as a sort of family. But the sitcoms boil down to something like this: all the characters are yearning for lives in which they'll share a deep intimacy with one other person.

As for me, I rule nothing out, but I'm definitely no longer a lady-in-waiting. And I do know this: Intimacy can result from being open to the world, not just to one other person.

To Wait or Not to Wait

Another year, another Valentine's Day, and still no sign of Mr. Right on the horizon.

Or even Mr. Half-Right.

It's odd, but Valentine's Day is beginning to affect me in the same way as New Year's Day. Which is to say: I find myself looking over the past year and assessing my life. In this case, my love life.

Right now, for instance, I'm trying to remember two things: The name of every man I've ever loved and the name of every man I ever *thought* I loved.

The first list is short. You could count the names on two fingers of your hand.

The second is long. Suffice it to say that for every Mr. Right, there existed a half-dozen Mr. Wrongs. When you're searching for a partner, it's so easy, isn't it, to re-invent a person into someone you could love.

Or, more to the point, into someone who could love you.

What I'm thinking about, this Valentine's Day, is that last bit: the urgent need we feel to be loved by someone. For the unattached person

— or, for that matter, the newly widowed or divorced person — it's the absence of feeling loved that's most painful.

And the fear of being alone.

A lot of women fear being alone. Or, more precisely, they fear being alone for the rest of their lives.

It's an attitude caught perfectly in a description by Doris Lessing of the unattached woman's response to men.

"A woman without a man," she wrote, "cannot meet a man, any man, of any age, without thinking, even if it's for a half-second, 'Perhaps this is the man.'"

And it's an attitude — if only a half-second attitude — that most women, regardless of age, have experienced.

What has become clearer to me over the last few years, however, is that I no longer have such an attitude.

I can't pinpoint the day or month or year when I stopped walking into a party with some vague thought that maybe this was the night I'd meet Him.

Which is not to say I haven't made the occasional inquiry, upon meeting an attractive man, as to whether or not he's married.

I have.

And they almost always are.

What's changed is that I'm no longer a woman who's waiting.

Throughout history, women have been consigned, by and large, to the role of waiting. Waiting for love. Waiting for marriage. Waiting for a house of their own. Waiting for children. Waiting for grandchildren.

We see the role that waiting has played in women's literature. Even the strong and lively women created by such authors as Jane Austen and Charlotte Bronte seem ultimately to have been waiting for marriage and their own household. Such books always end when marriage begins.

And we see the role that waiting still plays in the attitude of women and the subject of being single.

Or, as some would put it, of being alone.

True story: On a trip to Venice last year, I met a woman — a divorced novelist from New York — with whom I struck up a friendship. At dinner one night, she kept looking longingly at the nearby table where three couples were dining and laughing.

"Tell me the truth," she said as we were leaving. "Wouldn't you give anything to be like them? To be a part of a couple again?"

The truth? It had never occurred to me. I was having a wonderful time: The food was great, the conversation stimulating, and the view spectacular.

But my friend refused to believe me. In the end, Venice saddened her because she was not accompanied by a man who loved her.

In effect, I decided, she had chosen the "waiting" life. Even though she was traveling, her journey was essentially one in which she was "killing time" until her next marriage.

On the other hand, on this same trip, I also met a woman — once divorced, once widowed — who offers an instructive lesson in the richness of choosing a life free of "waiting."

Over the last dozen years, she has pursued her life alone with curiosity and openness. But she has not shut herself off from closeness or intimacy. "I haven't given up on anything," she told me. "I just don't sit around waiting for it to happen."

I like to think it's what I'm working toward: not giving up on closeness or intimacy, and being open to the world and anyone in it.

What I'm working toward, I like to think, is not giving up on anything.

Anything, that is, but waiting. ⊕

To Share or Not to Share

Other than a woman I know who says she's looking forward to her fourth marriage next month because she can't stand living alone, and the man in my fiction-writing class who told me he lives with his girl-friend because she does the housework, most single people I know break out in a cold sweat at the thought of living with someone.

"The problem is, we're all looking for just the right blend of intima-cy and autonomy in our lives," said a woman friend who's lived alone for the past 10 years. "And I guess what scares me about the idea of living with someone again is that there'll be too much intimacy and too little autonomy."

To share or not to share your life again — that is the question facing a growing number of men and women who now live solo, and who say they prefer it that way.

Gone — or almost gone — is the day when single people who lived alone, especially single women, were looked upon by couples as sad objects to be invited over for a home-cooked meal and matched up with unpromising blind dates.

And gone, too, is the mistaken idea that living alone is equivalent to leading a lonely life. Single people have learned the joy of solitude.

Now, in one of those modern twists, it seems single people worry not about living alone, but about whether they are capable of living successfully with another person.

Are they capable, for instance, of relearning a vocabulary that includes words such as compromise and accommodation and tolerance? Are they willing to relinquish some of the independence that living alone affords?

And they wonder about their ability to deal with the modern geography of intimacy: Will too much intimacy turn suffocating? Will too little intimacy prove disappointing? And what about those daily, minor irritations that have a way of accumulating like cars in a rear-end, pile-up collision? Can romantic love survive the pressures of real life?

"Only connect," wrote E. M. Forster, describing what is surely one of the most profound needs of humankind. And one of the most frightening.

91

Living together, sharing a real life — as opposed to a romantic fantasy — requires a lot of delicate negotiations. And it requires a willingness to allow the "illusion" of the relationship to be disturbed for something more substantial.

Of course, there are a lot of us who don't want the illusion disturbed.

From a single woman: "I don't want to be involved in all the domestic details and work pressures and annoying habits that come from daily contact. I'd rather have the fantasy."

From a single man: "I prefer being in a relationship where all I have to do is show up."

Most single people agree that a large part of the pleasure of living alone comes from the freedom to do exactly what you want when you want to do it; of being able to pick up and go whenever you feel like it.

Or as a female, forty-something colleague puts it: "The best thing about living alone is I can spend an entire Sunday in my nightgown eating popcorn without someone asking when I'm going to get dressed and what we're going to have for dinner. I can eat cereal for supper every night for a month. I can sleep when I like without worrying that someone is feeling ignored. What I fear most about living with another person is having to give up all these delicious little freedoms."

Of course, you could describe such freedoms as the small change of relationships. Still, a penny here and a penny there, and pretty soon you're talking the emotional equivalent of real money.

But the deepest fear among some single people seems to be this: that in sharing a daily life with another person — one that involves commitment, compromise and responsibility — they will lose contact with or have to deny a part of their real selves.

Perhaps, though, any small loss of the self can be compensated for by the intimacy that springs up between two people through sharing small moments: laughing at the same things, cooking a meal together, sitting in the dark listening to Mozart or the Beatles.

"What do I miss most living alone?" responded one single woman. "Not having someone to share Sunday mornings with." A male colleague: "The thing I miss most is hearing the laughter of more than one person when something funny happens."

Me? I miss not having anyone to slow-dance with at 3:00 in the morning when a disc jockey plays Ella Fitzgerald singing "My Funny Valentine."   ⊕

At the Beauty Spa

First came the nonalcoholic cocktails and iced shrimp, served in the peach silk and velvet drawing room. Then a butler rang a silver dinner bell summoning the two dozen women to the opulent, candle-lit table where Thanksgiving dinner was about to be served.

We were all strangers to one another — strangers who suddenly found ourselves gathered together to celebrate this most familial of holidays.

At dinner I was seated next to a woman wearing a small, diamond tiara who, without introducing herself, told me: "I've taken exercise classes from Jane Fonda. And I spend part of every summer at a spa in Switzerland. But I always come here for Thanksgiving."

Welcome to Thanksgiving at the Greenhouse — one of the world's poshest and most expensive health spas. Located on the outskirts of Dallas, this Rolls-Royce of spas caters to women only and usually is booked a year in advance.

Or at least that's what the voice on the other end of the phone told me when I called in August to make a reservation for October. "I'm sorry but we *could* book you in for October of next year," she said. After explaining that I was reporter who was coming to write a story on the spa, she relented slightly, saying: "Well, we do have a few openings for the week of Thanksgiving."

It was not exactly how I had envisioned spending Thanksgiving Day. But what the heck, I thought. It might be interesting to see who actually chooses to spend Thanksgiving at a spa. And, besides, there were plenty more Thanksgivings in my future.

So that's how it came to pass that nine years ago on Thanksgiving night I sat next to a woman wearing a diamond tiara who — between bites of an elegantly prepared 500-calorie turkey dinner — told me she always spent Thanksgiving at the Greenhouse.

But wait, you're probably saying, who goes to a spa for Thanksgiving? The short answer is: lonely people.

Some — like the divorced, 50ish woman from Alabama whose sons were vacationing with their father — were there trying to avoid the pain of not being with family.

Others — like some of the single, high-powered career women I met — were there because, as one of them put it, "It's a slow business week and the only time I can get away from the office."

And a few — like the tiara-wearing woman— simply traveled all the time, seldom staying anywhere for very long. Divorced with no children, she described her life to me one day over a low-cal fruit frappe, ending up with this summation: "But I've had a wonderful life. I really have. I wouldn't have missed it for anything."

But all the women — including the socialite from Houston who insisted, until almost the last moment, that she was there to rest up for the "Christmas party season back home" — were running away, more or less, from the prospect of being alone on this family-oriented holiday.

I know this because as the week wore on, the masks came off. And like girls at a slumber party or sleep-away camp, we'd sit around the potassium broth cart, talking, confiding, sharing. Or late in the evening, we'd meet in the Jacuzzi or at the pool for a swim and, without even being aware of it, we'd exchange some piece or another of the life we led away from the Greenhouse.

And by and large, I wound up liking — or, at least, understanding — many of my fellow spa guests.

Thanksgiving Day at the Greenhouse was to be the highlight of our week. The dinner was to be quite formal and elegant. And it was.

But whenever I think about that Thanksgiving dinner — and I do each year — the thing that stands out is how strange it all seemed. And how homesick I felt.

For if Thanksgiving is about anything, it is about family.

I remember calling home that night from the Greenhouse. Talking to my sons, I pictured what I heard going on in the background: the joyful noise of a family gathered together.

And I pictured the faces I loved: of my sons, of my mother, of family and friends. And I thought: Never again will I be away from them on Thanksgiving Day.

The irony, I suppose, is that I didn't stop to think that someday they might have to be away from me — that life would prevent some from returning home for Thanksgiving, as it has this year. And so would death.

But I will think today about all those I love — both present and missing — with the deepest of thanks. And maybe, for a split second, I will think about the lady with the tiara and hope she is not alone. ⊕

95

One of Us

Of the many things we know — or think we know — about Gloria Steinem, some items instantly leap to mind. For instance:

The image of a slim, youthful-looking woman who confidently marked her 40th birthday by telling admiring photographers, "This is what 40 looks like."

The image of a sexy, glamorous woman who never lacked for male companionship but chose, ultimately, to remain single, saying "A woman needs a man like a fish needs a bicycle."

The image of the hard-working, outer-directed feminist — an activist always on the go who maintained that "the examined life is not worth living."

And, judging from the face she turned toward the world, there seemed to be little in Steinem's inner life that required examination. Self-sufficient, self-confident, self-actualizing, Steinem seemed to embody the feminist ideal: a strong woman who had made choices about her life, rather than letting life choose for her.

In fact, for more than 20 years, Steinem has been so emblematic of the women's movement that, to the countless numbers of women whose lives she helped change, she is the women's movement.

Which is why many women may be surprised when they read Steinem's new book, which is, she writes, "the product of several years of therapy, of self-examination and 'insight' gained from a failed romance."

Come to think of it, surprised may be an understatement.

Perhaps the best advice for readers of *Revolution From Within: A Book of Self-Esteem* would be: fasten your seat belts. It's going to be a bumpy ride.

Jolt No. 1: For years, Steinem was simply "burnt-out." Suffering from feelings of "being neglected, deprived and insecure," she was a woman "turning away from a well of neediness that I feared would swallow me up if I admitted it."

Jolt No. 2: A few years ago, she came to a point where she was so "tired" and "depressed" that she "reverted to a primordial skill that I hadn't used since feminism had helped me to make my own life: getting a man to fall in love with me." And she says it's "alarmingly easy" to make a man fall for you, "providing you're willing to play down who you are and play up who he wants you to be."

Jolt No. 3: She chose a man with whom she shared few interests, enticed instead by his wealth and ability to shelter her in a time of extreme vulnerability; a man who "made every decision ... so all I had to do was show up, look appropriate, listen, relax at dinner, dance ... whatever was on his agenda."

But the biggest jolt of all is Steinem's description of a life not so much chosen as one driven by her bone-deep feelings of worthlessness. Inside the vibrant, confident woman, it turns out, there was a lonely, neglected child who needed to be recognized.

Steinem has told the story of her childhood before — the absent father, the mentally ill mother whose sole caretaker was her young daughter, the rat-infested house in which they lived — but until this book, it seems, the adult Gloria had never really connected with that child.

"I was fueled by insecurity," Steinem said recently on a radio talk show. "I was always driven by the need to help other women. I always identified with the victim without realizing it was part of me."

Her personal revelations have elicited mixed reactions, including expressions of confusion about what, if anything, it all means to the women's movement.

One critic, writing in the *New York Times* book review section, assessed Steinem's message this way: "It is an assertion of self-esteem as the driving force of the feminist movement and, indeed, of all positive social change — and as such, it provokes disturbing questions about whether this phase in Ms. Steinem's thinking is an advance or a retreat."

But some women found Steinem's imperfections reassuringly human: "To see that, like the rest of us, she is riddled with doubts and can still achieve is very heartening," one director of a university woman's study program said.

We all go through it: the struggle to deal with childhood ghosts, the search for a place to rest, the need to find out why we do what we do. And for each of us — man, woman and child — there are inner realities as well as outer realities. It's almost laughable to think it would be any different for a feminist.

In fact, you could make a case, as Gloria Steinem does, that she finally has located the missing half of the feminist equation: The political equals the personal.   ⊕

In The Garden

C ats, I have often observed, always look like they know exactly
where they're going and what they're going to do once they get there.

Dogs, on the other hand, frequently seem to be wandering about in
an aimless sort of way, just looking for the slightest distraction: an open
gate, a passing car, a leaf blown along by the wind. That sort of thing can
send a dog on a happy chase 10 miles out of his way.

Actually — and this is rather puzzling to me — what I really want
to tell you about has nothing at all to do with the philosophic differences
between cats and dogs and how they approach the meaning of life but —
for some reason — it's where this column starts in my head.

The truth is, what I really want to tell you about is an afternoon I
spent in the garden not too long ago. It was one of those unseasonably
warm, dappled autumn afternoons and Max (the cat), Fred (the dog) and
I decided to hit the lounge chairs in the garden for one last fling in the
sun.

Max and I made it to the chairs, but Fred was lost irretrievably —
for the afternoon, anyway — to the siren song of a discarded tin can

rolling along in the gutter, which, it now becomes clear to me, is why you had to sit through the first two paragraphs of this column.

Anyway, it was to be my favorite kind of Sunday afternoon — an afternoon of small pleasures: Max and I sitting together in a lounge chair (a vertical arrangement, of course, since cats never want to sit next to you if they can sit on top of you); a fresh croissant; a cup of strong, hot coffee; the Sunday paper; some puttering around in the garden; a brief nap drenched in the golden September sun, and, with any luck, a surprise cameo appearance by the neighbor's cat — an event guaranteed to provoke in Max a hilariously funny round of territorial strutting.

As I said, small — but wonderful — pleasures. At least to me. I guess I'm partial to small pleasures because they seem less perishable — more dependable, if you will — than the blockbuster pleasures: family, love, success, Pulitzer Prizes, and so on.

Anyway, what I'm remembering now is how I sank down in the chair with the kind of carefree feeling I used to have as a child when it was announced the whole family would be spending the day at the beach. This is more like it, I thought, as I watched a plumed gray shadow, a squirrel, leap like a miniature acrobat from tree to tree, its tantalizing nearness sending the cat into small paroxysms of helpless, twittering sounds.

So much was happening outside I didn't know where to look next, but I settled on watching the autumn sun hit the ground in slants of light, carving out intricate patterns on the grass, sort of the way light pouring through a venetian blind redesigns the patterns on a rug.

There was a lot of listening to do, too. I mean the whistles and calls, the chattering in the treetops — of squirrels and birds, preparing for the winter — filling up the air in a sort of free-lance autumn sonata, the disparate notes coming at you from all directions like an orchestra tuning up.

I wouldn't call what I was feeling that afternoon happiness exactly. It was something closer to simply enjoying things the way they are, not the way you want them to be. Totally unmotivated, my head absolutely free of paragraphs, deadlines and story ideas, I lingered all afternoon in the lounge-chair, dozing and smelling the faint aroma of burning wood in the air.

Then, as the light lost its transparency and moved toward the thickness of dusk, an odd thing happened. Half-asleep, I heard, or imagined I heard, a woman's voice calling to me across the garden, telling me to put on a sweater, reminding me that the sun was setting and it would grow cold. The voice called me Allie, as my grandmother did so many years ago in another garden.

Sitting upright and fully awake, I saw I was alone in the failing light. Alone, that is, except for the sudden feeling of a small, irrevocable loss. Of what, I'm not sure. My confidence, I think.

Whatever it was, the feeling matched exactly the abrupt sense I had of a chill in the air, and it sent me scurrying into the house to put on a sweater against the cold. ⊕

Unpacking A Life

Unpacking. That's how it started. Settling into her new home, the woman talked with her three friends as they stacked dishes, sorted linens, and got a little tipsy from the wine.

The woman's change in lifestyle had prompted old memories to surface, and she and her friends — helped along by the wine — talked freely about their work, their children, their ex-husbands, their current male friends, and how far they had all come, both personally and professionally, in the last five years.

"Face it," said woman No. 1 (the writer), "once you've enjoyed the freedom of living alone, you won't ever want to go back."

"Back to what?" asked woman No. 2 (the teacher).

"To Valium," joked No. 1, with a humor bred of unease.

"It's never having quite enough money and being with the kids all the time that will get you in the end," said No. 3 (the city planner and ex-rich wife).

"Yeah," said No. 1, "*you* get custody of the kids and your husband gets custody of all your old friends and their dinner parties."

The four women laughed, good naturedly.

They drank some more wine ("Hmmm," said No. 2, holding up the wine glass to the light, "1983 really was a good year for white jug wine") and then carefully began placing their friend's books side-by-side on the empty bookshelves which lined three walls of the room.

"Hey," said the teacher, holding up a copy of "Civilization and Its Discontents," "do you think Dr. Freud would get angry if I put him here, next to Gertrude Stein?"

"Put him next to Germaine Greer," said the woman whose books were being unpacked. "Maybe *she* can tell him what women really want." Pause. "I just wish I had a copy of Dr. Joyce Brothers' new book. That would give the good doctor a jolt. Her theory is that all men are just like children."

"Hold it," said the writer, her voice full of mock anger. "I think there's a *big* difference between men and children." Pause. "Children are much less critical of what you serve them for dinner."

"And a whole lot easier to live with," added the teacher.

"You're right," said the city planner. "Living as a single parent with children is a breeze — once you get used to all the modern inconveniences of trying to conduct a love life with short people constantly popping up behind you, in front of you, or beside you, asking you to play Monopoly." They laughed again.

Outside, the afternoon light was failing; inside, someone thought to light a fire, and the four women warmed themselves before it as they sipped their wine and talked of Jane Austen and Doris Lessing, of Emily Dickinson who, thank God, said the writer, "never had to read Gail Sheehy's dopey book, 'Passages.'"

Inevitably they fell to talking about money and success and of how they could get more of both. Happiness, they agreed, seemed out of reach. For the time being, at least.

And men. They talked of the kind of men who put in cameo appearances on birthdays and weekends — when it was convenient for them to do so — and called themselves fathers. And the kind who tried

103

to do more than that — really tried — but still wound up missing the rewards of sharing the ordinary, daily flow of life that marks and shapes a child's life at the deepest levels.

And they talked of life, vis-a-vis men, in the single lane.

"Good God," said the teacher, "whatever happened to *interesting* men? I went out with a guy the other night who spent an hour discussing the merits of the Ilie Nastase tennis shoe as opposed to the Stan Smith tennis shoe. It was, to be as kind as possible, about as much fun as listening to 'Bowling for Dollars' on the radio."

"Yeah, but the *really* boring ones, the ones you really have to watch out for," said the ex-rich wife (whose past life had acquainted her with more than her fair share of bankers and brokers), "are the guys who have first names that are really last names. Like Parker Prescott."

"Or Morgan Guaranty," said the hostess with a giggle.

The subject of loneliness and aloneness — two different states, they all agreed — came up. To one degree or another, they each had struggled with loneliness and attempted to make a separate peace with aloneness. Temporarily, they hoped.

And they all agreed that going to parties alone was easy; it was the leaving alone that was hard.

It was growing late and finally the woman whose life was changing stood up and looked around. "It really is a nice house," she said slowly, "but something is missing."

At that, the women fell silent and turned their attention to unpacking the boxes which held the past life of their friend. ⊕

ALICE STEINBACH

The Working Life

105

Well, here we are, almost at the end of the 20th century. And what a century it's been! In just under 100 years, the way we live and think has been altered almost beyond recognition. We have witnessed the advent of the automobile, mass production, voting rights for all Americans, moving pictures, psychoanalysis, television, space travel, computers, and the society-altering effects of feminism. And with each new development our lives have been dramatically changed.

Perhaps nowhere is the complexity of such changes more visible than in our working lives. Over the last 25 years, as more and more women moved into the workplace, we've seen major shifts in the structure of the family and the way men and women view one another. We've also witnessed a rising tendency to measure the value of a person by what he or she does for a living. Many of us do this: define ourselves through the prism of the workplace. Success on the job confers upon us the status of a valuable person; failure brings the opposite verdict.

The pleasure I derive from my own work is exceeded only by the rewarding labors of raising two sons. Parenting and working have a number of things in common. Both can be wonderful and awful. And both require a balancing act — just like everything else in life.

Having It All

N ot too long ago, I was interviewing an award-winning newspaper reporter about her career when, suddenly, she interrupted me with the following self-assessment about why she was so successful in her work:

"After two very short marriages, I began to think about all this creative energy you put into relationships — and for what? They were never satisfying or fulfilling for me. I never wanted children and so I figured what I ought to do is focus these energies onto something I do well. So I did. I focused them on work. To me, it was more satisfying than trying to split myself up between work and family."

I thought of her philosophy more than once during the last few weeks because, for the first time in a few years, I found myself in the role of a full-time mother again. With both kids temporarily living at home, there I was, back in the old Working Mother groove again, the perfect example of someone trying to balance the demands of work and family without shortchanging either.

And you know what? Even though my kids are older, I had almost forgotten how difficult and exhausting it is to be a Working Mother. I had almost forgotten just how fragmented the everyday life of a Working Mother can be. Because women — unlike men, who tend to take the office home — tend to bring the home to their office.

Anyone who has ever been a Working Mother — or sat next to one at the office — knows exactly what I'm talking about: the phone calls to the pediatrician; the phone calls *from* the pediatrician; the lunch-hour visits with teachers; the before-work test reviews; the after-work shopping expeditions; the midmorning drop-offs at school of forgotten lunches; the telephone attempts from the office to restore peace between fighting siblings bent on destroying each other and the house as well; the telephone linkups required whenever math homework is assigned.

And don't forget: In addition to all this, the Working Mother still must do whatever it is she does at the office.

Whew!

It seems to me that the true heroism of women lies not in "having it all" but in living through it all. Of course, more and more women are beginning to understand there's really no such thing as "having it all." At least, not all at once. The balance is constantly shifting, favoring this over that, that over this.

Still, the myth of the Superwoman Wife, Mother and Careerist continues. Take, for instance, this description in a recent magazine of a New York dress designer who supposedly has it all:

Working straight through lunch, she solved an accessorizing problem brilliantly. But the shadows were visible under her eyes. Between her days of work and her nights of charity events — and her persistence in waking up at 6:00 a.m. to practice piano — her life could be pretty exhausting.

Now, take a typical day in my own life when I was a Working Mother with two sons under the age of 12.

The alarm goes off at 6 a.m. No time for piano. Get up, dress, get the kids dressed, make breakfast, make lunch, drive the kids in car pool to school, arrive at work, sit down. The phone rings. A son has a stomach ache. Drive to school, pick him up, pick up babysitter, take them both home. Go back to work. Later phone rings again. Hard to make out what the voices are screaming on the other end of the line. Something like: "I'll kill him if he doesn't stop it." Have visitor in office so I politely reply: "Isn't that nice, dear. Thanks for calling." Hang up.

I could go on, but by now you either get my drift or you don't.

And, by the way, before you Working Fathers out there rise up in protest, let me say this: While it's true that more Working Fathers may be assuming the primary parental duties than ever before, it's still largely women's work.

Which brings me back to the last two weeks of my life and a return to the interrupted lifestyle endured by the Working Mother: the endless detours from all planned events, routine or otherwise; the fatigue of days that start early and end late; the pushing yourself to do what is beyond doing in a given day — and the deep satisfaction that comes when you get it done anyway.

Of course, all Working Mothers are fueled by a powerful emotion: love.

In fact, did I tell you about the time I was on the phone in my home office doing an interview with the great food writer James Beard when my nine-year-old son came on the line with his imitation of Julia Child giving her recipe for poulet in a basket?

James Beard loved it — he said my son had Julia Child's voice down to perfection. As for me, well, the reporter in me gave way to the mother: I loved it too. ⊕

The Opera Singer

At a small dinner party recently, the man seated to my left — a total stranger to me — turned and struck up a conversation by asking this question: "And what do *you* do?"

"I'm an opera singer," I responded, pitching my voice a bit higher than usual and affecting a French accent. "A soprano."

A few minutes earlier, I'd heard him asking the same question of a man seated opposite him. And a few minutes before that, I'd overheard him popping the question — "And what do you do?" — to the host's sister. Apparently the answers had not been the ones he wanted; he'd moved on quickly after learning one was a teacher, the other a social worker.

So when he turned to me, I was ready.

"An opera singer?" he repeated after me, his voice flushed with excitement and interest, his manner suddenly attentive. Mr. Johnny One-Note had finally found what he was looking for: A Trophy Dinner Partner. Which is to say, someone whose professional resume satisfied his need to connect only with those he viewed as successful and therefore worthy of his attention.

Whenever I get stuck next to this kind of dinner partner, I find myself longing to be at home, snacking on Cheez-its and playing Mousey, Mousey, Who's Got the Mousey? with an old washcloth and my cat, Harpo.

Question: Why do some people insist on thinking that a person is just a by-product of what he or she does for a living? That who you are is what you do?

Or vice versa.

But here's the worst news of all: Sometimes the person judging us in this manner is not someone sitting opposite us at a party or at work. It is someone sitting inside us: ourselves.

This need to measure the value of people, including ourselves, through the prism of the workplace is one reason why so many young adults emerge from high school and college in a semi-panicked state about their futures. They've seen the handwriting on the wall and it says: "You'd better pick the right career or you will never amount to anything in life."

111

Unfortunately, there's no postscript that adds: "On the other hand, you might think about deriving a sense of self-worth by balancing your life to include, along with individual work, the satisfactions of family and community and a connection to some larger value."

Few would dispute that we live in a very materialistic culture, one which offers rewards for how much money we make or what size house we own or how high we've climbed on the corporate ladder. And not so many rewards for satisfactions found in a life lived out in a somewhat slower lane.

Given such cultural standards — and don't kid yourself that adolescents don't see the one-upmanship that goes on among adults, including their parents — is it any wonder that young people often suffer from a lack of self-esteem and direction? Or that they see their future "success" largely in terms of acquiring the trophy house, the trophy job, the trophy husband or wife?

Of course, young people are not the only group who have limited access to the social affirmation that comes with doing something "important."

Women are quite familiar with the experience of being passed over socially because they're not "interesting." (*Read: They work at a low-profile job or don't work at all.*) For years, generations of women were judged primarily by what their husbands did. Now we have the interesting phenomenon of working women sometimes writing off non-working women as "uninteresting."

Often such "non-working" women are mothers who've made the decision to devote their energies to home and family. And although we pay lip service to the idea that nothing is more important than giving children a good start in a secure home, in subtle ways society downgrades the value of the full-time homemaker.

So, are you what you do? And if what you do is not deemed important by society, are you less valuable than the neurosurgeon, the judge, the university president?

It's your call, of course. Because the deep satisfaction that comes from honest achievement and a task well done lies not in our jobs but in ourselves.

By the way, the man at the dinner party, the one who still thinks I'm an opera singer, turned out to be a dentist.   ⊕

Rejection

Writers and lovers, I have often observed, have something in common: in the pursuit of their goals, both must be willing to face the terrifying possibility of rejection.

Of course, in the case of the rejected lover, usually the party doing the rejecting is smart enough to pull his or her punches, to dress up the rebuff in some flattering, verbal ensemble.

Example: "I'm sorry, Hugo, but this just isn't going to work out. You're just too smart and handsome for someone like me."

Or: "Alice, this has nothing to do with you, but I've decided to move to Nepal and become a Buddhist monk."

Then there's my personal favorite: "The easy thing, my darling, would be to try and make this work. But I know you're too courageous to do the easy thing."

Writers, on the other hand, seldom find their work rejected in such a silky, flattering way. They are more apt to get a letter that attacks the very thing that marks their work as uniquely theirs.

Consider, for example, the following letters of rejection to these then-unknown writers:

To poet Emily Dickinson — "Queer — the rhymes were all wrong."

To Gustave Flaubert, rejecting his novel "Madame Bovary" — "You have buried your novel beneath a heap of details which are well done but utterly superfluous."

To George Orwell, rejecting his book "Animal Farm" — "It is impossible to sell animal stories in the U.S.A."

But silky or sullen, rejection is still rejection. And no matter what anyone tells you, there are very few human beings who have mastered the art of being turned down. Which is unfortunate since, as we all know, life is 80 percent rejection, 15 percent acceptance and 5 percent undecided.

(The above poll, incidentally, is based on scientific research: I made up the figures and three of my best friends agreed with them.)

And since I was smart enough to fashion a life for myself that invites rejection at so many levels — writer, lover, parent, ex-spouse — I feel particularly qualified to make some timeless, although probably useless, observations on the subject.

First of all, it is important to recognize that you are the person responsible for inflicting a large percentage of the rejection on yourself.

Think about it. How many times have you critiqued yourself this way: I didn't get the job because I'm not smart enough. I got dumped because I'm not (select one of the following) sexy, interesting, tall, short, fat, thin, intelligent, or hip enough. My short story was rejected because I don't have anything to say and even if I had something to say I wouldn't say it well enough.

Such self-rejection accounts for approximately 75 percent of the total rejection in an individual's life. The remaining 25 percent comes from outside sources: spouses, lovers, bosses, head waiters, cosmetics saleswomen, health club instructors, people with good hair, mothers with children who behave, admissions officers at Harvard, and the *New Yorker* magazine.

A word about that *New Yorker* magazine rejection — which I received at the age of 18. Even now I remember the sting I felt when the

114

rejection slip arrived. I had submitted a poem which had as its central metaphor the interior of a rotting tree trunk. In sonnet form I compared this — the rotting trunk, weakened tree, etc., etc. — to the spiritual damage inflicted on society by greed and materialism.

As best I can remember, the rejection slip — which arrived almost by return mail — said something like this: "Your manuscript does not fit our needs at this time."

Of course, I immediately fixated on the words "at this time." Writers do that — search for, and find, positive messages in even the most blatant rejection.

Which, now that I think of it, is also true of lovers.

So, what have I learned from my encounters with rejection? One very important thing: That you eventually get over even the worst rebuff. Always, of course, just in time to move on to a new rejection.

Which brings up this question: Why is there so much rejection in the world? (80 percent, remember?) The answer? Because it's so much easier to reject things in life than to accept them. Acceptance, after all, implies commitment to a person or an idea or a poem about, say, greed and rotting trees. Rejection, on the other hand, implies the opposite.

By the way, did I mention that writer William Saroyan received about 7,000 rejection slips before getting his first piece published? Or that, when he won the Pulitzer Prize in 1940, he rejected it. The prize, I guess, did not fit Saroyan's needs at that time. ⊕

115

Success and Failure

It was a few minutes before air time and the talk show host was about to begin his daily radio program. He poured himself a cup of coffee and then, turning to me, said something surprising:

"You know, this job never gets any easier," confessed this erudite man who, for years, has presided over an extremely popular call-in show. "Every time I go on the air, I have to overcome a fear that I'll fail, that the show won't be any good."

He paused. "But I've found out something interesting about failing. And that is, you can build on success, but you really learn only from failure."

A few days later, a letter arrived that seemed, in a way, to continue this line of thought. Written by a young man I know quite well, the letter concerned itself with the idea that adversity might offer, in the long run, more rewards than getting what you thought you wanted. He wrote:

"What I guess I'm learning from my difficult situation is a deeper sense of who I am. And what I'm capable of when it comes to handling disappointment. I think — at least I hope — I'll come out of this a stronger person."

Then last week, in what seemed a curious completion of the philosophy lurking beneath both these remarks, I came across this unattributed
quotation in a book on mountain climbing:

"Today is a new day; you'll get out of it just what you put into it. If
you have made mistakes, even serious mistakes, you can make a new start
whenever you choose. For the thing we call failure is not the falling
down but the staying down."

Few among us can claim the distinction of not knowing the sting of
falling down, of "failure." The promotion not gotten, the honor not won,
the job lost, the praise denied — we've all known the loss of self-esteem
that comes with such moments. And because the wound of failure is a
deep one, we seldom risk sharing our feelings about such moments.

Which strikes me as unfortunate. Because when people are willing to
share such feelings, you can learn a lot. Listen, for instance, to this:

"Success does not necessarily build character — sometimes it doesn't
even build self-confidence," says a friend, one judged by the world to be
successful. "But most people I know can point to a disappointment or a
failure that resulted in what I would call a quantum leap of self-knowl-
edge *and* self-confidence. The confidence comes from knowing that you
can get through 'failure' and come out stronger on the other side."

Still, she admits it is a "painful process to go through."

Some successful people find that they become "addicted" to honors
and accolades. And when they don't get them, when they're just doing
well at their job — but not *sensationally* well — they feel depressed.

"It's taken me a long time to understand that prizes and honors,
while wonderful to receive, have a short shelf life," says one successful
journalist. "I have found that the sense of achievement you get from
'winning' needs to be constantly renewed. It's not winning that's hard.
But that's when you learn to dig deeper and do your best work. Not for
the rewards of success but for the rewards of self-respect."

Of course, you don't dig down to the level of bedrock he's talking
about without considerable blood, sweat, and tears.

A few years back, I found myself needing to dig down deep to find a

117

firmer foundation upon which to build my understanding of what success is and what failure is. And my friend was right: It is quite a painful experience to confront the loss of some trapping or another that seems bound up with success.

But eventually what emerged from the digging was a sense of something akin to freedom. A realization that there's a feeling of accomplishment and success that comes from mastering the pain of failure. And then getting on with the job.

Accolades are wonderful. Promotions are wonderful. Success — however you define it — is wonderful. But none of this, in my experience, really teaches you anything of lasting value about yourself.

Adversity, on the other hand, can be an inspirational teacher.

It is written somewhere that you stand on the summit for only a few moments; then the wind blows your footprints away.

Life's like that, too. The Harvard Business School probably doesn't teach that to its MBA's. But you know what? Maybe it should.　⊕

Second Acts

Along with choosing what kind of long-distance phone service to use, picking a career may be one of life's most confusing choices.

Partly it's confusing because such a decision is usually made at an age when you haven't a clue about who you are or what you want to do or what you're suited to doing.

And partly it's confusing because such a choice carries the burden of seeming to be an unchangeable, lifelong commitment. Once you've decided to become a lawyer, computer programmer or nurse, the theory goes, there's no turning back.

Ever.

It's an assumption that strikes terror into the hearts of college students — particularly as they approach graduation — and accounts for the dazed-looking faces you see on the nation's campuses this time of year. It's a look that says: "I'm scared and I don't know which is the right path to follow."

To which I reply: There is no right path and the sooner we all learn this, the better off we'll be. There are many different paths by which we may arrive at our desired destination — and while a straight line may be the fastest route, who's to say it's the most interesting or productive one?

Actually, I think the concept of going through life — professionally speaking — in a lock step, linear march toward the top of the career pyramid has a lot in common with being locked onto a six-lane interstate highway with no exits between the beginning and end. Not only is it boring, but it deprives you of the opportunity to explore all the interesting geography that's hidden from those who travel only the main roads.

My own job resume, for instance, reads like a poorly thought-out itinerary to no particular destination. But despite that, I think I've managed to get, more or less, to where I've wanted to go. And enjoyed getting there.

It's an attitude which my friends with incredibly well-constructed resumes tell me is risky. And it is. On the other hand, it's beyond my scope to imagine taking a job you have no interest in solely because it will advance you toward your goal.

A word of warning, however, about traveling this way: It takes longer. And the risk of failure is greater. Greater, that is, if you define failure as being willing to stop doing something — even if you've been doing it well — to do something new and unfamiliar.

Still, this willingness to take a risk on something new can work out quite well.

Take, for example, the case of writer Tom Clancy, whose novels have all been best-selling blockbusters. Although making a very successful living as an insurance agent, Clancy felt, in his words, "stuck in a boring job." So he took a detour — decided he could always get back on the main road if things didn't work out. Of course, in his case — as anyone who's read "The Hunt for Red October" or "Red Storm Rising" knows — things worked out pretty well.

One of my favorite examples of someone who came late to her profession and persevered in pursuing what she once called the "second act" of her life was actress Ruth Gordon. She was in her middle 40s when she started in films. At the age of 72, she won her first Academy Award (best supporting actress for "Rosemary's Baby").

I often think of her acceptance speech when I talk to people who say they're washed up professionally at age 50. Or derailed at age 30. Or passed over by their company at age 40.

"I can't tell you," said Ruth Gordon to the wildly cheering Hollywood audience, "how encouraging it is to win this."

On the other hand, we have no less than F. Scott Fitzgerald, whose writing career plummeted from brilliant beginning to failed ending, warning us: "There are no second acts in American lives."

I suppose such a judgment might be borne out nowadays in the failed comeback attempts of such aging athletes as Jim Palmer, Bjorn Borg, and Mark Spitz. But second acts, in my opinion, should not be confused with second chances and the wish to return to what you once were.

Second acts are not about going back; they're about going forward. They're about finding something new in yourself as you grow older.

121

Of course, it's hard to convince a young person that the career choice he or she initially makes is not a fatal — or final — decision. But part of maturing is learning that life is confusing and inconsistent. On the other hand — and to life's great credit — it is seldom unchangeable.

So I say: Bring on the second act. And let it be full of surprises. ⊕

Still Betty After All These Years

I t's probably just a coincidence that in 1963 these two major events occurred: Betty Friedan's revolutionary book "The Feminine Mystique" appeared; and the popular television show about the ideal family of the 1950s, "Leave It to Beaver," disappeared.

Nonetheless, coincidence or not, it is tempting to look back and see symbolized in these two events an important turning point in the evolution of a woman's place in society.

Of course, of the two, it was Friedan's book that altered the social landscape, changing the way we live and the whole trajectory of relationships, families, politics and the workplace. "The Feminine Mystique," in the opinion of sociology professor Amitai Etzioni, is "one of those rare books we are endowed with only once in several decades, a volume that launched a major social movement."

This comment from Professor Etzioni comes straight from *Playboy* magazine, the issue just out that features an interview with none other than the founding mother of contemporary feminism herself, Betty Friedan. And in this so-called Year of the Woman, it seems appropriate to revisit the woman whose recharting of the social map set a new course for our society.

It's also appropriate — and necessary — to remind ourselves exactly what it was that Friedan did.

It had nothing to do with bra burning or reviling men or abandoning families. What Friedan did was to tell women everywhere that the problem they suffered from — "the problem that had no name" — resulted from a society whose social, educational and commercial pressures had created a harmful discrepancy between what women really are and what they are told they should be.

For those of you who are too young to remember, I'll just insert one little example of what society's male-dominated attitude was like back in those days: In 1956, *Life* magazine interviewed five male psychiatrists, all of whom declared that female ambition was the root of mental illness in wives, emotional upset in husbands, and homosexuality in boys.

In those days, the ideal woman was a version of June Cleaver: the "happy Mom" who not only was always there for Dad and the kids but, more important, embraced such a role as the only role for women. The premise put forth by Friedan's book — that it was alright for women to want more than just the June Cleaver role — was, and continues to be, the most hotly debated issue surrounding feminism.

123

Friedan revisits the issue in the *Playboy* interview, saying: "I never believed that feminism was opposed to family. Feminism implied an evolution of family. Feminism was not opposed to marriage and motherhood. It wanted women to be able to define themselves as people and not just as servants to the family. You want a feminism that includes women who have children and want children, because that's the majority of women."

It is this sort of observation by Friedan that has met with hostility from some younger feminists, including Susan Faludi. Faludi, the author of "Backlash," has accused Friedan of damaging the feminist cause by suggesting the women's movement was failing because "its leaders had ignored the maternal call."

It is a charge Friedan answers this way in the *Playboy* interview: "Faludi is right that the backlash has undermined much of the progress we made. But the answer is not to ignore [the fact] that most women want families. The women's movement started with many women who already had children and didn't want to be defined solely in those terms."

It's an interesting observation — that many of the women who started the movement were mothers. And it may account, in part, for some of the tension between older feminists and younger feminists. Among those younger women who want but have not yet had children, some of the toughest decisions — or choices, if you prefer — lie in their futures.

And I'm willing to bet that no matter what track these young mothers choose — the stay-at-home track, the Mommy Track, the fast track — they will feel some guilt. Which is why it's important for women to support and respect one another's decisions. Whatever they may be.

Or as Friedan puts it: "I am against polarization of women against women, whether it comes from Dan Quayle or Susan Faludi or Camille Paglia."

No doubt about it: Still Betty after all these years. ⊕

On Assignment

A few days ago, as I was standing in the drugstore reading Mother's Day cards and wishing I still had a reason to buy one, I suddenly heard a voice call out from behind me.

It was the voice of a young boy and it said, with a certain childish urgency, the following word: *MOM!*

I recognized the voice as that of my 10-year-old son and, instantly, I felt my mood change from one of vague homesickness to one of cozy familiarity. So much of what was good about my life was conveyed in that voice, in that one word: Mom.

One thing puzzled me though: How did my 10-year-old son manage to track me down and find me in that drugstore? Especially since he's now 21 and a college student in New England.

I spun around and found myself face-to-face with a boy who clearly was somebody else's 10-year-old son. And yet ... the boy's voice, his face, the way he walked by his mother's side — not holding her hand but clearly linked to her in ways less visible but far deeper than hand-holding — all these things together evoked the image of my own son at that age.

I watched as the boy steered his mother toward the candy counter. I listened as he filled her in on his day in school; eavesdropped as words that telegraphed a whole way of life drifted over to me — words like *Dad* and *soccer* and *carpool* and *birthday party*. His mother listened, her manner alternating between attentiveness and responsiveness, the perfect maternal combination.

For whatever reason (and I suspect there was more than one), I was vulnerable to this brief conversation between mother and son, an exchange as slight in its way as a wind-driven ripple on the water's surface. And yet, as solid as a rock.

Driving home from the drugstore, my thoughts wandered about, pausing briefly at the doorway leading to memories of my own two sons, then moving on to an incident having to do with other sons, other mothers.

It happened one night while I was working on a newspaper story about a homicide detective; a story that required spending a few nights hanging around with this detective while he worked the streets.

The two of us went into some neighborhoods that I found intimidating. At one point, for reasons too complicated to explain, I found myself separated from the detective and left stranded briefly with a group of street-smart adolescent boys.

It was a little before midnight and we were standing outside a bar on a downtown street. The boys were vying to impress me — a reporter earnestly writing down their words — with their toughness, telling me story after story of how aggressive they could be, how cruel they could be, and how little there was in life they valued.

Of course, what was not said was how little there was in life that valued them. Family was a foreign concept to all of them. Most lived a life that did not include the notions of carpools or birthday parties. Or Dads.

The boys were eager to have their names appear in the newspaper, and the tougher the image they cast, the better. Toughness, in their world, was hard currency; it could buy you an identity, a sense of self. Self-esteem even.

Then something happened; that small, illuminating detail that reporters are always looking for — the journalistic equivalent of the psychoanalytic insight, I suppose you could call it. A car swerved right in front of us, just missing a thin, frightened dog who was running across the street. The dog, whimpering and pathetic-looking, headed straight for us.

And suddenly, these tough guys turned into the boys they once must have been. Or could have been. Or maybe still were underneath the swaggering veneer so carefully built-up over the years.

One picked up the dog, cradled him, told him not to be afraid. Another boy went into the bar to buy a hamburger for the dog. A third gently stroked the dog, muttering something about how the dog should-n't worry anymore; they'd take care of him now.

From somewhere within, these boys retrieved, for a little while at least, the instinct to nurture. I wondered how long it would be before life on the streets closed down that instinct.

The point is, we know life can be brutal and dehumanizing, and it shouldn't surprise us when we encounter people who have become bru-tal and dehumanized.

What surprises me is how even the toughest cases sometimes manage to keep a small, tender flame going inside.   ⊕

ALICE STEINBACH

Growing Up

129

In dreams, the spring winds blow through my childhood. Through my grandmother's garden and the back porch trellised with morning glories, they blow; along the downtown streets where I walked holding my mother's hand tightly until we got to the Century movie house, they blow; down the winding steps to the neighborhood library and the lady who told stories, they blow; then the winds rise up to the top of the trees I walked through on my way home from school; they blow past the black-and-white-spotted dog who barked at me, past the corner grocery store where I bought snowballs in the summertime, and past the house of my best friend, Ducky Harris.

In the Kingdom of Childhood, I reigned. It all comes back to me in dreams and in memory, details as vivid as a red rose: how I felt, what I saw, who I was. That girl is never far from me; the connection is like that between stem and flower, all of a piece, one holding the other up, one allowing the other to bloom.

In dreams, spring winds blow, and the clocks I hear at midnight are the clocks of my childhood.

Counter Culture

I don't know about you, but I love drugstores.

Let others search for the perfect French restaurant. Let others seek out the latest "in" spot for an elegant Sunday brunch of champagne and eggs benedict. Me? I'm always looking for a certain kind of drugstore, one with a long counter and a row of high stools with chrome backs and fake leather seats which swivel around just enough to let you squeeze in and climb on.

Actually, I don't think I've ever met a drugstore I didn't like. There's just something about the smell of scrubbed marble counters, the sight of towering chocolate cakes under glass domes, and the fragrance of coffee brewing on an open burner that never fails to make me dizzy with longing. For what, I don't know.

What I do know, though, is that one of my most stubborn fantasies, dating back to a time when most of my life lay ahead of me — and what didn't was comprised mainly of plans and daydreams about the future — involved owning a drugstore.

Or, to be more precise, owning Lowe's Drug Store.

When I was 12 and poised in that awkward and seemingly endless space just between childhood and adolescence, I spent a lot of time sitting at the counter of Lowe's Drug Store, which seemed to me easily the most exciting place in the neighborhood. It had everything.

For instance, I'm remembering what a good place it was to spend a hot, sticky August afternoon, the kind of afternoon that threatened to go on forever. It was always cool in Lowe's (the only other air-conditioned place was the movie house two doors down from Lowe's and, face it, how many times can you stand to see Charlton Heston in "The Ten Commandments"?). Armed with a notebook and pen, I would spend such a summer afternoon drinking vanilla Cokes and watching the other customers, pausing now and then to write down some random observation. (I always took care to prop up an open book against the thick, green Coke glass, hoping that no one would notice I never turned the pages.)

And I'm remembering the perfume counter just to the right of the door as you walked in; the thick crystal bottles, fluted and filled with amber liquid which gave off hints of grown-up secrets and had names like exotic thoughts: Tabu, Evening in Paris, Jungle Gardenia (my personal favorite) and White Shoulders.

And just now I'm remembering how much I liked the way they decorated Lowe's. Seasonal. In February, there were lacy, cut-out hearts and boxes of chocolates shaped like valentines and wrapped in layers of red cellophane and taffeta ribbon. Easter brought big, woven baskets filled with tiny chicks of marshmallow and chocolate eggs and candy bunnies as big as the real thing, all nestled on a bed of shredded green paper grass. And Christmas. Well, I don't have to tell you about Christmas, the crepe-paper Santas, and the way the counter was strung with long, cardboard cutouts of reindeer pulling a sleigh.

But most of all, I'm remembering Nettie. Nettie waited on the counter at Lowe's. I soon found I could talk to her in a way that eluded me with most other people. Two or three times each afternoon, Nettie would take a break and ease herself onto the stool next to me at the end of the counter. She'd pull out a Lucky Strike cigarette, light it up and exhale the smoke through her nose.

Then we'd talk about all the things that really matter, from her troubles with Roy, her boy friend, to the state of my hair and whether I should let my bangs grow out. Nettie showed me how to paint my nails with Revlon's Fire and Ice, and she helped me pick out my first sympathy card from the rack, tactfully steering me away from my first choice — a large, lavishly flowered card which said, as I recall it, "My deepest sympathies go out to you and yours in your time of need" — to something more modest.

At first, she made fun of my notebook and constant scribbling, but later she would say something and finish the thought off with, "And, honey, you can write that down." If I didn't — write it down, that is — she seemed almost hurt, as though what she said hadn't been important enough to merit attention. She'd rephrase what she said until I made some notes.

A few years ago, I drove out to the old neighborhood, searching for the large teardrop-shaped globe — the color of a clouded ruby — which hung over the entrance, just under the sign that said "Lowe's Drug Store." A laundromat is there now.

But the odd thing is that I know exactly what Lowe's would look like now: There would be a back-to-school theme and all the counters would be filled with spiral notebooks and leatherette pencil cases and fat rubber erasers. And somewhere at the end of the counter, Nettie would be sitting next to a young girl, the two of them talking a blue streak. ⊕

133

Camp Baltimore

Out of the corner of my eye, I saw her last week: A laughing girl, about 10 years old, walking in a circle of friends toward the neighborhood schoolhouse. She was half-skipping with excitement and carried in her hands, instead of books, a bouquet of garden flowers.

Small details, perhaps, but to me they conveyed a big message: School was about to shut down for the summer.

The last day of school! When you're 10 years old, are there five sweeter words in the English language?

Remember how the air suddenly seemed lighter on the day that school stopped? And how — now that you could sleep later — you didn't mind getting up earlier? And how you felt flooded with a sense of freedom now that summer stretched out endlessly in front of you, like an ocean with no visible shores?

It all came back to me in a rush last week — fueled by the sight of the girl with the bouquet and, later that day, a visit to my old summer camp.

Which, by the way, was located in downtown Baltimore.

Actually, when I was growing up, downtown Baltimore *was* my summer camp. And there was no better place in the world, I thought then, for a 10-year-old to enjoy summer than in the city.

In those days, it was easy to get downtown — the streetcar ran almost from the front door of my house into the heart of the city. And there was always the hope that — if luck was on my side — I might catch one of the old, red, double-decker buses that still ran up and down Charles Street. Even now, when I think about it, I relive the thrill of climbing the little circular stairway that led to the upper tier of one of those buses.

My typical summer day would begin at 9 a.m. when I met my best friend Constance at the downtown YWCA. Our mornings were spent in tumbling classes, tap dancing classes, and swimming in the large indoor pool. Before entering the pool area, we'd go to a small room where an attendant handed us drab, tank-type bathing suits in sizes that never fit.

The pool at the Y dominated the building. Although it was located in the basement of this seven-story building, the chlorinated smell from the pool hung like a veil over every floor. There was a wonderful sense of never being far from some body of water. It was a feeling complemented by the cool, damp, tile floors throughout the building; every time I walked on them I thought of the pictures I'd seen of tiled Roman atriums with splashing fountains.

At noon we'd leave the Y and walk over to Reads Drugstore for lunch. To get there we had to navigate the two-block area that comprised Baltimore's Chinatown. The trip past the mysterious-looking restaurants with their pagoda-shaped facades always sent a slight shiver through us; we automatically quickened our pace.

About a block away from Reads, you could start to smell the fragrance of roasted peanuts, the free ones being handed out by a man dressed in a peanut costume. We'd usually eat the hot, salted nuts sitting at the counter in Reads, waiting for our grilled cheese sandwiches and cherry Cokes.

After lunch, we headed over toward one of our favorite places: the

135

children's reading room at the main branch of the Enoch Pratt Public Library. We'd take a shortcut by walking through an alley where a number of flower wholesalers had shops. Clay Street, as the alley was called, always smelled of roses and gardenias, and the alert pedestrian could be certain of finding discarded but still beautiful stalks of gladiolas along the curbside.

Over on Mulberry Street, after a quick stop at the Carry-On Thrift Shop to browse among the antique jewelry and beaded evening bags, we'd walk down the flagstone steps to the courtyard entrance of the children's reading room. There, we'd spend a few hours reading on our own or listening to the daily "story hour" presided over by a beautiful, red-haired librarian with a special fondness for the Grimm Brothers' "Twelve Dancing Princesses."

At about 4:00 in the afternoon, we'd head for the air conditioned comfort of Kresge's five-and-dime store, where we'd listen to a piano player in the sheet music department play the top songs of the day.

Then we'd head back up to Charles Street to wait for the streetcar, often getting caught in a brief summer downpour. I see it now: the cars splashing through the rain, the hot raindrops hitting the asphalt streets and sending up an instant smell of damp heat.

Such are the memories of my summer camp: Camp Baltimore.

Sibling Rivalry

I am told by a family member that when I was five I had to be physically restrained from throwing myself in front of a new two-wheel bike my older brother was riding. The emotion behind this semi-Tolstoyian gesture was not, however, the suicidal despair of an Anna Karenina but the juvenile jealousy that drives children in their early years.

My brother was given the shiny black bike for his eighth birthday and I — mad with jealousy because I was allowed only to ride a tricycle — planned to call attention to the unfairness of the situation by flinging myself under its wheels.

The plan, alas, backfired when my mother pulled me out of harm's way.

Such an incident, of course, is all too typical of the sibling rivalry that runs like a river through the landscape of childhood.

And while such feelings date back at least to Cain and Abel, suddenly the idea of re-examining the impact of sibling rivalries is a hot new topic. At least three self-help books addressing the subject are out, or due out, this fall.

In a review of one such book, "Mixed Feelings: Love, Hate, Rivalry and Reconciliation Among Brothers and Sisters," the book's author, Francine Klagsbrun, comments on the lingering effects of sibling rivalry, saying: "If you felt you could never compete with your older brother, you're probably going to have a hard time getting a promotion at work, because deep down you feel like you can't make the grade."

I was quite surprised to read this since my own experience completely contradicts such a notion. The fact is — despite my feelings of being unable to compete with an older brother — I once received a promotion at work. In 1978.

And believe me, I have never felt that just because I drive a six-year-old Honda and my brother drives a brand-new, shiny, black Schwinn — I mean, Mercedes — that he's making the grade and I'm not.

But look, nobody ever said science couldn't be manipulated — just like younger sisters — to produce a desired effect. So one must take such observations with a grain of salt.

However, for those of you who are not as sure of your own unconscious motivations as I am, here are three questions to ask yourself to determine if you're still competing with a sibling:

1. Have I been taking tennis lessons twice a week for the last 25 years because of a buried wish to beat a sibling just once in some contest?

2. Am I stockpiling money so that the nursing home I enter 40 years from now will be a fancier nursing home than that entered by a sibling?

3. Did I blow up last year at the family Christmas party because Mom gave a sibling better toys — I mean, presents — than she gave me?

And speaking of Mom, did yours have a stock line when you complained that a sibling was getting better treatment than you?

Something along the lines of: "You should be ashamed of yourself for thinking that a shiny, black, two-wheel bike is a better present than paper dolls. Don't you know that children in India don't have paper dolls?"

Or: "So you didn't get a shiny, black, two-wheel bike! Big deal! As long as you have your health you shouldn't complain."

Or: "You should be thankful you have feet to pedal that tricycle, young lady!"

Growing up, I always thought that as you grew older and more secure in your accomplishments, you would see how foolish an emotion jealousy is. Such a belief, by the way, accounts for why so many of us are willing to attend our high school reunions.

Which reminds me: Did I imagine it or did it really happen that at my last high school reunion, four friends and two teachers asked me for a detailed accounting of my brother's life since high school?

I suppose that no one is immune to feelings of jealousy. Still, I expect that some of us pick occupations that offer more opportunities for comparing one's work to another's, with this result: Jealousy.

Writers, I think, fall into this category. Dentists don't. Dentists, I believe, seldom look into the mouth of a new patient and think: "Holy Toledo! I've never seen such incredible crowns! They make my crowns look like a joke! Who am I kidding? My older brother was right. I should have gone into real estate."

And speaking of real estate, did I mention that my brother lives in a house three times the size of mine? Or that it has a swimming pool? No big deal, of course.

I mean, look: I still have feet, and children in India still don't have paper dolls. And I say, as long as you have your health, what's to complain about? Certainly not a shiny, black, two-wheel Schwinn bike.   ⊕

Christmas

While walking alone at night through the neighborhood, my intention being to admire the wreaths and trees and candles shining in windows, I hear a door open and out spills the sound of Bing Crosby singing "White Christmas."

A woman appears briefly, a cat runs outside, the door closes.

Through the window, I watch as the woman walks back into a circle of light, back into the room decorated with fir and red flowers and lit candles. She hangs an ornament on the tree.

I walk on: Past the house whose dozens of windows frame tiny, flickering candles; past the porch where Santa sits in his sled; past the giant wreath that frames an entire doorway; past all the windows through which I can see signs of Christmas.

I walk on: Above me, I hear the wind moving through the trees. I breathe in the clean smell of air fragrant with coldness. Looking up, I see the flying horse Pegasus galloping across the winter sky.

I walk on: A stray hemlock branch brushes my cheek. A man carrying bright red shopping bags, two in each hand, passes me. "Merry

Christmas," he says. And just as I turn to head home, a black cat with yellow eyes springs out from behind a row of hedges. He leaps onto the hood of a green Buick parked nearby.

A memory springs out with him. And suddenly I see another cat, another green car, and another Christmas.

Now I'm remembering driving at night along slick, wet streets, the car's headlights shining two small circles onto the iced blackness of the road ahead. It's freezing outside and heat is pouring out of the little vents in the dashboard, causing the windows to fog up. Enclosed inside this small cubicle of warmth and light are just my father and me.

The radio is on and the words "Away in a manger, no crib for a bed" fill up the car. From the window, I watch the houses go past in a blur of colored lights and electric candles. Once in a while, if I refocus my eyes, I see myself reflected in the icy window, an eight-year-old dreamer, dreaming of Santa Claus and Christmas morning.

And now I'm remembering how when we got home, my cat jumped down from the window sill and ran across the grass to meet us. It is a clear, moonlit night and I can see tiny beads of ice clinging to his gray fur. And with each of his elegant steps, I hear the crunch of a paw breaking through the thin crust of old snow.

Inside the house, there is more light and warmth and, later, tucked into my bed, I hear the voices of the adults downstairs.

As I listen to them through the half-open door, the sounds blend into one voice.

It floats up to my room: up past the pictures of my grandparents that line the stairway wall; up past the banister my brother and I slide down every morning; up past the hooked green and white rug where the cat sleeps; up past the cushioned alcove where I read my Nancy Drew books.

Outside, I hear the ice creaking in the fir tree and someone calling in his dog from the wintry night: "Here, boy! Here boy!"

A slight movement of my blanket tells me the cat has jumped onto my bed. His paws smell of the damp earth; his fur smells of wood smoke from the neighborhood chimneys. His yellow eyes glitter in the dark like bits of gold confetti.

I lie in bed imagining what they look like, my family, sitting downstairs in the living room, the lights of the tree blinking off and on behind them.

I imagine how surprised my mother will be when she opens her present: a crystal powder box for her dressing table.

I imagine what my presents will be. A gold locket, I hope. And a pair of roller skates. Maybe a powder blue sweater.

Remembering all this now, as I walk at night through the stillness of the neighborhood, I think: Something is stirring in me. What is it that I seek in such memories? What is it that I want returned to me?

I turn to the black cat with yellow eyes who still waits patiently on the hood of the green Buick. I lean over to stroke his fur. It smells smoky and cold, and suddenly I find what I am looking for: A link to the child I once was.

Finding that, I feel happy. Finding that, I feel connected. Finding that, I feel excited.

I walk on, the black cat following me.

"Merry Christmas," I call out, although no one is on the street.

No one, that is, but me — both past and present.   ⊕

Prom Night

I would like to say that I kept my mouth shut because, after all, the three teen-age girls trying on prom dresses at the mall were total strangers to me. But after 20 minutes of watching them debate the merits of the green silk vs. the deep red taffeta, I became so involved I could stand it no longer:

"Buy the white silk crepe with the spaghetti straps and get a pair of high-heeled, white satin sandals!" I blurted out to one of the startled girls. "Wear long, crystal earrings and pile your hair up on top of your head like Brigitte Bardot," I advised another.

I'm not sure they had the faintest idea who Brigitte Bardot is and they certainly didn't know who I was, but for some inexplicable reason the three high school seniors seemed not to resent my brief intrusion into their world. In fact, they even allowed me to hang around their dressing room to talk prom dresses, hairstyles, and the pros and cons of false eyelashes.

I loved every minute of this brief regression; it was like being back in high school with my best girlfriends. In fact, I liked it so much that driving home from the mall, I decided that the strapless red taffeta was the perfect prom dress for me. Perfect except for one thing: My mom would never let me get away with that low, V-shaped neckline. I would have to do some pretty fast talking to get it by her.

It was at this point that I realized I was being sucked into the Black Hole of Senior Prom Memories.

Prom Night Redux: I'm 17 years old and by three in the afternoon I've already laid out everything I'm going to wear to the prom — from the strapless, white silk dress to the Merry Widow longline bra that cost almost as much as the dress.

Mom, who would have preferred I wear a high-necked, long-sleeved dress made of sackcloth or some other non-clinging fabric, had fought me tooth and nail over both the dress — "too tight, too sophisticated, too much" — and the Merry Widow bra — "too tight, too sophisticated, not enough" — but finally, out of sheer exhaustion, gave in.

But to tell the truth, I secretly agreed with her. The outfit wasn't me. It was too daring; a distinct departure from my usual sportier approach to fashion, one that was patterned — quite unsuccessfully, I might add — after the models I saw in the *New Yorker* ads for a store called The Bermuda Shop.

I had discussed some of my fears about this new look with my three best girlfriends one day after lunch period. The four of us were sitting outside, smoking extra-long Pall Mall cigarettes in a clear space under a huge, overgrown bush. It was an offense — smoking on campus — that was punishable by suspension, and usually we didn't take such chances. But the closer we got to graduation, the more reckless we felt.

Maybe, unconsciously, we even wanted to be suspended; wanted something to happen that would stop our forward march away from childhood and toward the uncertain future facing us. And maybe this leave-taking of the past that had nurtured us — or, in some cases, not nurtured us — also accounted for the ease with which we all wept that spring before graduation.

It was a time of high emotion. For example, I remember so well sobbing aloud a few weeks before graduation when my English teacher read Keats aloud: "A thing of beauty is a joy forever: Its loveliness increases. It will never pass into nothingness." Looking around the room — this was an all-girls' school — there wasn't a dry eye in the house.

Of course, passing into nothingness wasn't our only fear. There was also the horrible possibility that our date for the prom would show up smelling like Juicy Fruit gum and wearing a powder blue tuxedo with white patent shoes.

But he didn't. He showed up looking like a movie star — a strangely exotic figure in evening clothes who bore no resemblance to the 18-year-old boy who hung out on your back porch all summer long.

The night was a blur of dancing and laughter and romantic songs played by a fancy local band. At one point, my girlfriends and I gathered in the hotel's elegant "powder room" to exchange gossip. And there among the silk chairs and softly lit mirrors, we wept and vowed to keep in touch for the rest of our lives.

And we have. Why, just two weeks ago, I ran into Rachael from my high school class. Of course, we hadn't seen one another for decades, but I distinctly remembered her prom dress. "It was white tulle and the prettiest one of all," I told her.

Rachael broke the news to me gently:

"It was blue. And it was satin." ⊕

145

Piano Lessons

I guess the first person I ever heard playing the piano was a guy named Manny who tickled the ivories in a supper club called the Algerian Room. He must have been forty-something. I was five.

I got to know Manny because the Algerian Room was tucked away in a corner of the hotel where my Aunt Claire resided. And sometimes, if I was very, very lucky, a visit to my aunt's hotel would end up with the two of us sitting on fake zebra-skinned banquettes listening to Manny as we waited for our steak sandwiches; she, drinking her Manhattan and I, sipping my Shirley Temple through a thin, blue cellophane straw.

I remember it as thrilling: the mirrored bar; the dim, bluish light; the tall, frosted glass that held my Shirley Temple. But most of all, I remember the way Manny played; the way the sounds seemed to spin around the room and bounce off the walls, right into my body. I felt like a tuning fork.

Oh, sure, I had heard piano playing on the radio, and had listened to bad renditions of "Danny Boy" as played daily by our next door neighbor, but never until Manny had I understood the power of the piano.

Sitting at a shiny black baby grand under a red velvet canopy, his fast, elegant hands hitting the keys only a few feet away from where I sat, Manny made me suspect there might be a difference between something called sound and something called music.

For reasons known only to my unconscious, Manny was very much on my mind last weekend when I set out to buy a piano. For years, I've been promising myself that I'd resume taking piano lessons and now, I'm really going to do it.

Interestingly enough, it turns out that I'm on the cutting edge of a trend.

According to the Trendsters — those folks who measure each tiny, social tremble in the culture — more and more adults are taking piano lessons. One piano teacher in Brookline, Mass., calls the increase in adult students an "explosion"; one that's got parents vying with their kids for music teachers and practice time on the old piano (a development which could usher in the phenomenon of the "two-piano family.")

147

As a trend, experts say, taking piano lessons is going to be right up there with getting braces on your teeth at the age of 40.

The truth of this was driven home last week when a chat with a neighbor yielded the news that his wife, a recent convert to piano lessons, was at that very moment in the house practicing. Wow! I thought. For the first time, my neighborhood is at the forefront of a trend!

Well, anyway, in anticipation of the new, second-hand piano arriving at my house, I went down into the basement to retrieve some old music books that belonged to a son. Instead I found Miss Pearl Evans, my old piano teacher.

Her ghost was there on every page of my worn copy of Ravel's "Interlude Moderne," the piece I played at my first — and only — piano recital. Marked in Miss Pearl Evans's spidery handwriting were notations such as: *More emotion. Faster. Softer.* As I glanced over the music, I found my fingers striking the notes in the air.

Funny, it doesn't seem all that long ago when as a kid I'd take the streetcar from my home to the "Studios of Miss Pearl Evans." (Nobody ever called her "Miss Evans." It was always "Miss Pearl Evans.") Of course, there were no studios; just a living room — empty except for a piano and a few straight-backed chairs — situated at the front of her small house.

She lived alone and, as far as I could tell, her whole world revolved around her students. I remember sitting in her dining room — which served as a waiting room — listening to the kid before me struggling through some piece of music that was always totally unrecognizable to me.

One summer Miss Pearl Evans took me and two other students to see a movie called, "A Song to Remember," the story of Chopin's life. After the movie, we all went to the Arundel ice cream parlor and over chocolate sundaes served in silver dishes, talked about the sacrifices Chopin made to achieve his artistry. I went home that night vowing to practice at least 20 minutes more every day.

Of course, I didn't. But now I have another chance.

And by the way, did I tell you I also retrieved from the basement a small bust of Chopin given to me by Miss Pearl Evans? I plan to put it right on top of my piano when it arrives. Now if I could only find a bust of Manny.　⊕

Girls to Women

Somewhere in the back of every woman's mind — perched just beneath all the tumultuous, boy-obsessed, peer-driven, body-conscious anxieties associated with adolescence — lies the separate image of the free and unmuddled pre-adolescent girl who came first; the one who existed before hormones, self-doubts and the arduous, adolescent task of breaking away from one's parents took over and changed everything.

At least that's the picture suggested by a non-scientific but rather spirited survey of several of my women friends.

This friendly survey, I should point out, was prompted by a recent article in the *New York Times Magazine*, which explored the sharp contrasts between the way 11-year-old girls and 16-year-old girls view the world. Its conclusions were telegraphed in the brief but compelling headline accompanying the story:

"Confident at 11, Confused at 16."

Without exception, all of my friends admitted reading the headline and experiencing the shock of recognition — *self*-recognition. And judging from subsequent letters to the magazine, it seems to be a fairly universal response — one summed up in this letter from a woman in West Bloomfield, Mich.:

"My own 11th year has remained vivid throughout my life. I remember telling myself these exact words, 'I'm 11 years old, in the sixth grade, and the world is beautiful.' I had the confidence that I was a very smart girl, that I would know how to handle any situation, and that I would create my own world. And then there are the four decades that followed."

With the exception of that last, sorrowful thought — which we will get back to — the letter strikes a definite chord in the women of my survey. And me.

At the age of 11 — we remind one another over a dinner called to explore our feelings on this subject — we were solid in our friendships; confident in school. We felt uneclipsed by boys in sports or academics. And our self-esteem definitely did not depend on what boys thought of us.

And at 11, we were reading books about strong, independent, curious women: Nancy Drew, Jane Eyre, Queen Victoria. We put on plays in someone's club basement and played all the roles — male and female. Saturdays, we descended on the YWCA, where we spent the day swimming, tap dancing, and taking gymnastics classes.

And most of the time we supported one another and cheered one another on. Of course, there were occasions when jealousy and anger intruded, but only briefly. The argument passed, the insult faded, and we proceeded to march on together, a little phalanx of 11-year-old girls, confident about our place in the world.

Looking back, we agree — but not until coffee and dessert arrive — that our world at the time may have been narrow, but it was a world that seemed to welcome us.

It was a lot harder to agree about what exactly changes girls.

In the *New York Times* article, which is based on a five-year study headed by Professor Carol Gilligan of the Harvard University Graduate School of Education, Gilligan locates the source of the change to that time in adolescence when "girls come up against the wall of Western culture, and begin to see that their clearsightedness may be dangerous ... in consequence, they learn to hide and protect what they know ... to think in ways that differ from what they really think."

None of us was sure of Gilligan's precise meaning — except for the part about thinking in ways that differ from what you really think. But our feeling was that the inability to break away from the iron grip of peer pressure and assert one's individuality is the very essence of adolescence — and the heart of the problem under discussion. That and the urgent, confusing, sometimes miserable, but ultimately wonderful task of locating one's place as a sexual entity.

And finally we wondered: Isn't it just as likely that boys are also confident at 11 and confused at 16? And isn't that something we all have to live through until we come out on the other side and find ourselves back on the road to confidence again? (A rerouting which sadly did not seem to happen to that letter-writer from West Bloomfield, Mich.)

On that note, the evening ended. And as we all spilled out of the restaurant, shouting goodbyes, what I saw was this: A laughing phalanx of middle-aged women, each one ready to take on the world with all the confidence of an 11-year-old girl.   ⊕

151

The Mocking Birds

Although it may come as something of a shock to those who know me only as a journalist, I was once rather well known as a star pitcher for a now-defunct baseball team known as the Mocking Birds.

As a matter of record, I won 10 out of the 85 games I pitched in my first year with the team, a statistic which caused me to consider seriously a career in baseball, dismissing entirely my mother's suggestion that a girl of nine ought to keep her professional options open.

What I had going for me, as I recall it, was an unusual underhand curve ball. Although poorly executed (it earned me the nickname "The Pretzel") and entirely dependent on dumb luck (I threw it a different way each time), I have to admit it was an eye-catcher and responsible for a remarkable number of strikeouts, chiefly because the batter was frequently doubled over with a severe case of laughter.

This halcyon period in my baseball career lasted long enough for my reputation to spread throughout a 12-block area, a circumstance which I took every possible advantage of. But, as is so often the case with halcyon periods, the end of it and my baseball glory days came about rather abruptly.

If you asked me to pinpoint exactly when it was that my promising baseball career started to unravel, I would have to say it was in the spring of my 11th year when my older brother Shelby, who was managing the Mocking Birds, traded me down to the Gnats.

(To give you an idea of the quality of the Gnats, I would simply point out that Reds, a rather dilapidated neighborhood Golden Retriever, was often pressed into service as catcher for the team.)

That was also the spring when the lilacs bloomed for two full months. A spring for lilacs, people went around saying, like no other they could remember. Some combination of rain and sun and temperature or just luck, they said, caused it. Whatever was behind it, I still remember standing on the pitcher's mound with the purple and whiteness and perfume of the lilacs all coming together, blowing in from somewhere off right field (probably from Mrs. Cox's garden) all spring long.

Early summer, however, brought an end to the lilacs. And to my pitching career. The end came in the form of relief pitcher Bebe (Gabby) Foster.

New to the neighborhood, Bebe just showed up at the field one day, and pretty soon I began thinking of her as Bebe-the-threat. My brother, a manager who knew raw talent when he saw it, made up his mind that she was in and I was out. As a pitcher she not only had "good arms" but good other things, too — things which, for a girl of 11, were precociously developed.

When my usual, reasoned approach to dealing with my brother failed (I threatened to tell everyone his middle name was Henry), I was sent down to the Gnats. But I'd be lying if I told you that my spirit wasn't broken. Pitching to a Golden Retriever takes it out of you.

Years later, in what I suppose the Freudians would call an act of sublimation, I decided to try my hand at sports writing, a decision which led to my meeting Reggie Jackson.

Although I can't claim to know Reggie Jackson well by any means — or at least not as well as I will lead my grandchildren to believe —

I did get to spend some time with him in 1980 during the five-day, star-wars series between the Yankees and the Orioles. It was my first sports assignment, and I knew it was my big chance to make a name for myself in sports writing. (The name I had in mind was Red Smith, but he wouldn't let me use it.)

It was a plum assignment. With one *little* hitch. Reggie Jackson wasn't giving interviews. To anyone. Undaunted, I got a pre-game press pass and trotted out to Memorial Stadium on a Thursday evening armed with a tape recorder, notebook and about 70 pencils, hoping that once I saw him on the field I could somehow talk him into an interview.

The pre-game scene at the stadium that night was wall-to-wall reporters, all waiting for Reggie. He appeared at about 6:30, an hour before game time, causing a reportorial stampede in his direction — one in which I arrived almost first. Just as I was about to approach him, a female reporter from a New York paper practically knocked me to the ground, a move which sent my notebook and tape recorder flying into the air. "Puh-leeze wait in line!" she explained. "Do you *moind?*"

Perhaps out of pity — who knows? — Reggie, who turned out to be a nice, bright guy, came over to me, listened, and agreed to an interview. (Alas, after lunch with Reggie and his sister the next day, he decided it was all to be off the record.)

Still, that evening, after setting the interview date, I left Reggie to the hordes of reporters and wandered out to the pitcher's mound, delirious with dreams of glory. And although it was August, not spring — standing there, just 60 feet away from home plate, the wind blowing in softly from right field — I remembered the year of the Mocking Birds, and I swear I could smell lilacs in the air.   ⊕

ALICE STEINBACH

Daily Pleasures

Various art, film, and television critics at certain newspapers have told me more than once that it's far harder to to write about something they like than something they don't like. Or as one such writer put it, only half-jokingly: "I don't know anything about what I like, but I know a lot about what I don't like."

When it comes to the matter of enjoying life — not Life with a capital "L" but life as it's really lived, from day to day, carpool to carpool, meal to meal — most of us tend to adopt the critic's stance. At every opportunity, we spot easily the things that annoy us, bore us, displease us. We also seem able to identify the big, glittering, and inevitably unreliable Pleasures in Life: a beach house in Malibu, winning the lottery, or landing the job of our dreams. No problem.

The trouble begins when we try to recognize the small, dependable pleasures that come and go in the flow of daily life. Often they remain a blur. We're too focused on the annoyances in the foreground to see the quiet delights in the background. The son calling down "Good night, Mom!" from his bedroom. The snowdrops pushing their way through the hard, January earth. The baby who smiles at us from his perch in the supermarket cart.

156

Train yourself to see such small moments. At the end of the day, they're what you'll remember.

One Moment in Time

Lounging in my lawn chair one recent Sunday — the newspapers   **157**
stacked up next to me, a cup of hot coffee at hand, the cats arranged in
comma shapes on the grass, the sun dappling the leaves in light and shade
— I thought to myself: This is it. Pure happiness.

Not the blockbuster kind of happiness that we spend so much time
searching for in love, marriage, work, success and a good haircut — but
the smaller, more dependable happiness that lies coiled, just waiting to be
sprung, in ordinary moments.

Part of the happiness I felt this recent Sunday had to do with the
knowledge that I didn't have to be anywhere at any given time and that
no one was waiting for me to produce something. But part of it was
even simpler than that: It had to do with my willingness to simply enjoy
things the way they were, not the way I wanted them to be.

Still, I found myself thinking: If happiness is as easy as that — some
free time combined with a mind open to the moment — why is it so
difficult to stay happy over a long period of time? And so easy to stay
sad? Is there something about the human condition, I wondered, that

directs us away from being happy? Or is it that we have a tendency to misunderstand the nature of happiness — to think of it as a permanent resident in our lives, rather than a visitor who comes and goes.

The notion of happiness as a permanent state of mind is reinforced in a recent issue of *Self* magazine. In an article which asks and answers the question "Who's Really Happy and Why," psychologists and surveys tell us there are individuals who fall into the category of "happy people." Not people who have happy moments, but people who live in a condition of happiness.

And, according to the article, there are also specific groups of people who exist in a "happy" state. The hierarchy of happiness, they say, goes like this: "Women are, on the whole, happier than men ... married women the happiest group of all, followed by married men, unmarried women and unmarried men."

Trying to pin down who's happy most of the time and who isn't seems a fool's errand — based, as it is, on the assumption that happiness exists as an ongoing emotional trait.

But happy moments — those moments when you feel fully alive — certainly exist. They swim by us every day like shining, silver fish waiting to be caught. Interestingly, what I hauled in anecdotally on the subject turned out to be the small fish of happiness, not the big denizens of the deep.

Or as one woman put it: "The weird thing is that the big things I always expect to make me happy never really do. It's often little, seemingly inconsequential things that do it for me. Over the weekend, for instance, I went to my mother's for dinner and she made mashed potatoes. I hadn't had mashed potatoes in months and when I saw this lumpy, misshapen mass on my plate, I was thrilled."

Here, then, from my own fully unscientific survey of friends and colleagues, is the catch of the day — happiness-wise.

Happiness is:
• Coming home and seeing the light blinking on the answering

machine.

- Triumphs by my kids, triumphs by me.
- Thinking about the first time someone told you they loved you.
- Long driving trips with someone you're completely comfortable with.
- Long driving trips by yourself.
- A phone call late at night from someone you were thinking about and hoped was thinking about you.
- Blue Mountain coffee, freshly brewed.
- Seeing someone you love after a long absence.
- Waking up without the alarm.
- Waking up to the smell of bacon.
- A guy who says "I'll call you" and actually does.
- A good perm.
- Getting flowers at work.
- Making coffee for a guy after a good date.
- Having your hair washed by someone you love.

Random observations, yes, but with some connecting threads: love, hair, unstructured time, and coffee.

But, ultimately, what's so wonderful about happiness is that even when you're not searching for it, it can find you. How else to explain the feeling I had a few days ago when a boy of about two came up to me in the supermarket and told me he liked my shoes.

I felt happy. ⊕

Camelot

So another day dawns and, as usual, things get off to a rocky start:

You get up to find there's no hot water and your cat is sick and needs a trip to the vet but you can't take him because you've got to be at work by 8 a.m., so you're going to have to take him when you get home at 7 p.m.

If, that is, he's still alive.

Next, you find out that your automatic garage door won't work, which means you have to climb in through the garage window and operate it by hand from the inside, a tricky maneuver which causes you to throw out your chronically bad back.

This, of course, comes after the telephone call from your out-of-state son informing you that a financial emergency has occurred and unless he can find someone to lend him $300, he may have to quit eating for a month.

And on top of all this, no matter what you do with your hair — mousse it, spray it, blow-dry it, iron it, curl it — it still looks awful.

So, you're probably thinking, what else is new? Who doesn't know that the days when nothing goes right outnumber — by about a billion to one — the days when all things do?

Point well taken. But once in a great while, we chance upon a day when the heavens come together, the stars align themselves, and the gods conspire in such a way as to give us a day in which everything goes ... *right!*

Such was the case for me last week when, for one brief, shining day, I stumbled by accident into Camelot.

It began with a good-news phone call from an out-of-country son. He'd just learned the job he'd pursued for months was his. Talking to him, I suddenly became aware that over in the corner, Max, the old, arthritic cat, was acting like a kitten, playfully leaping into the air in pursuit of his younger brother, Fluffy. For the first time in months, Max ate his breakfast with gusto.

Arriving at the office about an hour later, I was surprised to find a check in the mail — payment for the reproduction rights to an article I'd written 15 years earlier. That little development was followed by a phone call from another son who announced he'd been accepted — after months of anxiety on both his part and mine — into graduate school.

Walking to the cafeteria to get my second cup of coffee, I noticed my back didn't hurt. In fact, it felt great. It was almost too good to be true — all this in one day. *Plus* my hair looked terrific.

It made me think about other days like this, days so full of good news and unbridled hope that, despite their brevity, you never forget them.

My first day in Manhattan as an art school student was one such day.

From the moment I stepped out of my fifth-floor, walk-up apartment — armed with a sketchbook and a *New Yorker* magazine — to the end of the day when I heard Charlie Parker play jazz at Birdland, I walked surrounded by a halo of youthful optimism.

My teachers liked my work, I liked my teachers, and on the way home from class, I found a part-time job at a small art gallery in the Village. Was there anything left to wish for in the world? Not really. But

161

such fine days have a pattern of their own: Celebrating my good luck at Schrafft's soda fountain that afternoon, I actually sold a sketch — for $3 — to the woman sitting next to me.

All that *plus* my hair looked good that day.

But Camelot never lasts. In this case, it departed abruptly the next morning when I awoke with the chickenpox.

So, yes, I knew last week that my state of carefree happiness was temporary.

I knew that the cat would languish again, that the sons would face disappointments, that the surprise checks would fail to arrive in the mail, that my back would hurt once more.

And I knew, with certainty, that my hair would once again look awful.

But standing outside my kitchen door that night — the night of the day when I dwelled briefly in Camelot — I knew also how important such days are.

They made the stars seem brighter, somehow. And the air softer. They made the sounds of water from a neighbor's garden fountain take on the clarity of crystal.

And standing there, I realized how constricted the senses can become when held captive to the stress of always trying to stay ahead of something — without even knowing what that something is.

But here, on this singular day, life had freed me briefly from all that, and I knew it. For the first time in a long while, I caught the scent of rain in the air and noted how quickly the clouds can move by even when there's no wind in the air.   ⊕

Mail Chauvinist

F ew things in life can so consistently rouse hope in me as the
arrival of the mailman at my door. It doesn't matter that the reality never
lives up to the expectation: That more bills arrive in the mail than
checks, more bedding catalogs than love letters, more solicitations than
felicitations.

The plain truth is: Regardless of how bad my mail may be today, I'll
wake tomorrow with renewed optimism. Mailwise, that is.

Yes, I admit it: I am a mail chauvinist. And I am not alone. There are
millions of us: mail chauvinists who run to our mailboxes every 10 minutes to check the contents.

We live for the samples of breakfast cereal and dish detergent that
arrive in cunning little packages. We thrive on the envelopes that promise
us — if we'll only open them — an island in the Caribbean or
$1,000,000 in cash. We pin our hopes on what's inside the large hand-
addressed manila folder with no return address on it.

"Make my day!" is what we mail chauvinists think when we see the
familiar flash of that blue-gray uniform turn the corner and head our

way. For us, it's the high point of the day; the reason why we keep on keeping on in this crazy world that doesn't amount to a hill of beans.

And it's the reason why there was a flood of protests last week when the U.S. postmaster general talked about the possibility of cutting out residential mail deliveries on Tuesdays and Thursdays.

In other words, what those lunkheads over in Washington were suggesting is this: that the postman always ring twice — less a week.

But the postmaster general had not counted on a public outcry in response to his trial balloon. In fact, the response was so great that the day after he floated this dopey idea in the newspapers, Mr. Postmaster General went on record as "remaining committed to six-day delivery."

Some may say, "So what?" But I say: This is one giant step for man-and-womankind. The fact is, there are so few things left for man-and-womankind to feel hopeful about that just knowing the mail thing isn't going to be taken away makes me feel more hopeful about the future of the planet.

To drive home my point — which in case you've forgotten is that mail represents the triumph of hope over experience — let's examine the contents of my mailbox today. It includes:

A very exciting large envelope emblazoned with the return address of the John D. and Catherine T. MacArthur Foundation. This is the foundation, you'll recall, that awards "genius grants" of many thousands of dollars to really smart people. Talk about hope! But, alas, it turned out to be a newsletter on population explosion. Still, at least I now know the MacArthur folks have my name and address.

Next in my mail is a white, letter-sized envelope addressed to me. Printed across the top of the envelope is this message: "A remarkable new book about the Steinbaches is about to be published — and you, Alice Steinbach, are in it!" Next to the message is some sort of baronial-looking crest with the name "Steinbach" printed under it.

Inside is a letter telling me that a new book, *The World Book of Steinbaches* — probably the German spelling of my name — "is about to be published and it is being offered to the 1,526 households bearing the

Steinbach name in the world." I immediately sent off my $10 deposit.

Next are two invitations to a son —who lives abroad and has autho-rized me to open all his unimportant-looking mail — to sign up imme-diately for $10,000 worth of credit. No questions asked.

I, on the other hand, receive an invitation to reserve in advance a funeral plot. Perpetual care offered.

There is, of course, the usual bundle of catalogs and magazines. Today's sample includes one for *Difficult to Find Tools*, one for *Solutions to Your Chronic Back Problems*, and the always welcome *Cats of the World Digest*, which this month features sledding Bavarian kittens on the cover.

And last but not least in my mailbox today is a postcard from Seattle. I turn it over eagerly and read the bold, flowing handwriting: "Seattle is beautiful. Already I've found an apartment, a job and some peace of mind. I hope you have thought over our conversation and will come to your senses. I love you." It was signed, "As ever, Stan."

My heart beats wildly at the thought that Stan, as ever, loves me. Then I see who the postcard is addressed to: someone named Sue Sweeney. ⊕

News of the World

Last week, the weather in Osaka, Japan, was dismal: muggy, in the 90s during the day and dropping down only to the low 80s at night.

Out in Boulder, Colo., though,the weather was glorious last week: dry, sunny days in the 90s followed by nights that dipped below 60.

And across the Atlantic, the temperatures in Copenhagen were exactly what the travel books describe as normal for that city in late August: overcast skies with occasional sun and a high of about 68; then nights that hover around the 50-degree mark.

For the last two months, I have traveled daily from Baltimore to Osaka, Boulder, and Copenhagen. First, I stop in Boulder to visit a son, then on to Osaka and another son, and finally to Copenhagen for a brief rendezvous with a close friend. I make the entire three-city trip in five minutes.

Which is about the length of time it takes to open my morning paper to the weather page and travel down the listings to each of those cities.

Actually, scanning the weather reports takes only about one minute;

the other four are spent in the service of establishing a daily connection with three people who loom large in my life but who, for the time being at least, loom large from a distance.

Sitting at my breakfast table, weather maps in front of me, I imagine them in their individual settings: one rising at daybreak to the sight of the Rocky Mountains under pale blue skies and fading stars; another walking through the thick, humid air of a Japanese night scented with quince; and the third setting out under cloudy skies, headed for a late lunch in Tivoli Gardens at a lakeside cafe.

I should add, however, that not all of the material in these morning reveries comes from the daily weather reports; much of the detail has been supplied through a rather out-of-date medium: the letter. Each of the scenes described above was first described to me — vividly — in a letter.

It's an interesting experience, this business of letter-writing as the main form of communication between you and those you are separated from. Although it lacks the immediacy of a telephone call and the very real pleasure of hearing the other person's voice, I am discovering that old-fashioned letter-writing — which is to say, trying to keep up with another person's life through correspondence — has its own unique rewards.

Someone once described the material that emerges from a consistent correspondent as an "unself-conscious autobiography," one in which the writer expresses his hopes and dreams, his fears and disappointments. Unlike the telephone call in which the physical voice is present, the inner voice is often what one hears in a thoughtful letter.

A friend writes to me, for instance, about the death of someone close to both of us: "Death ends a life; it does not end a relationship."

It's not the sort of thing you would verbalize, even to a friend. But you could write it.

And a grown-up child writes to a mother about a new way of seeing her — the words-on-paper expressing unspoken feelings:

"This morning I awoke with an image, a memory of you in your blue leotard and tights, dancing in the living room the last night I was home. When I was watching you, I suddenly saw you before you met Dad, before you had two children. For once, I didn't see you as the parent or the wife, but as the woman, yourself. You were yourself, dancing in the living room, spontaneous, full of life."

I remember the postcards and letters that used to arrive during temporary separations — hasty notes that would say things like: *Dear Mom, This is a really exciting trip. Yesterday, we were the last group allowed to canoe through the fires in Yellowstone Park.*

Or: *Dear Mom, I love New Orleans! Last night, Rob and I had dinner with a family of gypsy fortune tellers we met on Bourbon Street. It was great!*

And I remember the countless letters from a passionate Italian friend that always began and ended: *T'amo! T'amo! T'amo!*

No longer so hasty or so passionate, the letters arriving now bring news of lives that, wherever they might be lived, are contained in my own.

One night after reading a letter from Japan, I opened the back door and the damp, rose-scented air spilled into my kitchen. It carried the scent of Japan. And it carried — air-mail, so to speak — the image of a far-away son. ✷

Friends and Recipes

N ot too long ago, on a night when I couldn't sleep, I wandered
downstairs into my kitchen looking for some mindless diversion.

Instead I found myself reliving the past.

It happened as I was foraging about in my pantry and discovered an
old, wooden box of recipes on the shelf, right behind the Chocolate
Chip Breakfast Bars. Inside the little box, I found a part of my life I had
almost forgotten, one that dated back to my high school days when I first
discovered the pleasures of cooking.

There, neatly typed on 3-by-5 cards or scrawled on the backs of
envelopes or scraps of yellowing paper, was a kind of history of my life.
Or at least a part of it.

I recognized my mother's handwriting on the three-card-long recipe
for an English trifle, the one she made each Christmas; another, a recipe
for super fudge cake, was written in a bold, artistic hand and signed, like a
painting, by my friend Ellen.

I laughed out loud when I got to a recipe I had clipped out of
Seventeen magazine many years ago. It was the first cake I ever baked

completely on my own, and to honor such a momentous event, I had crossed out in ink the name given the cake by *Seventeen* and renamed it "Alice's Mystery Mocha Confection."

I sat there studying my handwriting on the card and it was as though time fell away; I could actually *remember* writing the words *Alice's Mystery Mocha Confection.* It was odd: For just a moment, looking at my prim, precise handwriting, I could see without any obstruction the link between the sleepless woman sitting in the kitchen and the girl flushed with success, renaming the cake.

There are many ways, I suppose, to review a life: Reading old letters or looking at family photo albums is guaranteed to stir up the sediment of old memories. A number of my male friends tell me that sports is the straw that stirs the past for them; that the merest mention of, say, the year 1956, followed by the name Mickey Mantle, plunges them back into the thicket of strong, shared experiences.

Sports, of course, are known to be one of the great bonding experiences among men. It occurred to me the other night, as I leafed through the cards and worn, folded bits of paper, that the exchanging of favorite, closely guarded recipes is a similar experience among women; that the listing of specific ingredients in a recipe is not unlike the sports statistics men rattle off so easily to one another. Both represent, I think, a sort of shorthand language that's a crucial part of the bonding experience.

Most of the recipes in my file are titled with the name of the person who was generous enough to share an admired concoction with me. *Gloria's Bread Pudding; Marion's Lemon Icebox Cake; Katherine's Hot Mulled Wine.* They're like chapters in the book of my life; the memories associated with each name are part of the narrative that's formed my story.

A few of the recipes, however, retain an air of mystery. There is, for example, a recipe written in pencil under a masthead that reads: From the desk of David Lloyd Kreeger. Two questions arise: Why do I have a recipe from the desk of David Lloyd Kreeger, an internationally known art collector? And just what is it a recipe for? There are no instructions or names given — just a list of ingredients.

With the exception of Kreeger's mystery contribution, all of the recipes used to be staples in my cooking arsenal. And — don't laugh at this — I actually used to answer my kids' question about "What's for dinner?" by replying, "Margaret's pork chop casserole" and "Marion's sour cream coffee cake."

I've always felt a bit sad that I have no daughters who might carry on the tradition of recipe-sharing. I suppose that's why I felt particularly heartened when a son recently wanted a copy of one of my recipes for his girlfriend. "You know, Mom," he said over the phone, "the recipe for 'Leslie's best fudge we ever ate.'"

It was always one of his favorites.

ELLEN'S SUPER FUDGE CAKE

2 cups sifted all-purpose flour
1-1/2 teaspoons baking soda
1/2 teaspoon salt
2 cups sugar
4-1/4 ounces unsweetened chocolate
1/4 pound (1 stick) butter
1 cup boiling water
1/2 cup sour cream (heaping)
2 eggs
1 teaspoon vanilla
1 tablespoon mocha flavoring

171

1. Heat oven to 350 degrees.
2. Grease and flour 8-inch or 9-inch cake pans.
3. Sift together the flour, baking soda, salt and sugar in a bowl.
4. Melt the chocolate and shortening in the boiling water. Over low heat, stir until blended, then remove from heat and cool.
5. Pour chocolate-butter mixture into a mixing bowl. Add sifted dry ingredients. Blend.

6. Add sour cream gradually while beating (medium speed if using electric mixer). Add beaten eggs. Add vanilla and mocha flavoring.

7. Pour batter into greased and floured pans. Bake for 25 or 30 minutes, or when toothpick comes out clean. Remove from oven. Cool in pans 15 minutes, then remove to wire racks.

8. If desired, use a medium angel food cake pan and bake for about 45 minutes.

9. Ice as desired. Thin dark chocolate glaze recommended for tube cake; thicker chocolate icing for two-layer cake.

GLORIA'S BREAD PUDDING

3 slices bread, more if desired
2 eggs
pinch of salt
1 teaspoon baking soda
1 teaspoon vanilla
1/4 teaspoon each cloves, cinnamon and nutmeg
3/4 cup of sugar
1/2 cup milk
extra milk to cover bread
butter
nutmeg

1. Heat oven to 375 degrees. Set cake pan half-filled with water in bottom of oven.

2. Butter a 1 1/2-quart ovenproof casserole. Place bread slices in bottom of casserole.

3. In a bowl, combine eggs, salt, baking soda, vanilla, cloves, cinnamon, nutmeg and sugar. Add 1/2 cut milk and stir. Pour on bread. Cover bread with more milk 'til it's covered. Sprinkle with nutmeg and dot with butter. Bake 35 minutes. Serve hot or cold.

4. If more bread is used, increase the amount of vanilla to taste.

MARCIA'S ARMENIAN CAKE

2 cups light brown sugar
2 cups pastry flour, sifted
1/4 pound (1 stick) butter
1 beaten egg
1 teaspoon nutmeg
1 teaspoon baking soda
1 cup sour cream
pinch salt
cinnamon
4 ounces chopped pecans

1. Heat oven to 350 degrees. Grease a 9-inch square pan.
2. In a bowl, blend sugar, flour and butter, cutting butter into dry ingredients until mixture is crumbly, as in pie dough. Divide the mixture in half. Spread half in pan.
3. To remaining dough in bowl add egg, nutmeg, soda, salt and cream. Beat well. Pour onto mixture in pan. Sprinkle with cinnamon and chopped pecans.
4. Bake 40 minutes without opening oven. Cool in pan. ⊕

ALICE STEINBACH

Daily
Afflictions

Daily afflictions — or as I like to think of them, the annoying detritus of daily life — come in various forms and from disparate sources. Waiting for the plumber to arrive, balancing the checkbook, fielding phone calls from various long-distance phone companies, making trips to the post office for stamps, particularly on any day of the week between 8:30 and 4:30 — all such activities fall into this category.

Of course, there is no daily affliction quite so bad as that inflicted by someone or something you come into contact with on a more-or-less daily basis: The spouse who whistles constantly while driving in the car. The cats who get angry if you forget to leave out their catnip toys. The close friend who insists on telling you the truth about your hair color. The cats who will only drink water from the Ming Dynasty bowl inherited from your mother-in-law. The son who eschews Healthy Choice frozen dinners and demands a salad and fresh fish instead. The cats who insist on sleeping across the heat vents in your bedroom with little or no regard for how cold some other people sleeping in the same room might be. The cats who ... oh, well, I think you get the picture.

Deconstructive Criticism

A mong the many hard lessons to be learned in life are these: that success does not bring happiness; that there's no such thing as a free lunch; that it is better to look good than to feel good; and that, ultimately, nobody gets out of here alive.

But the hardest lesson of all to learn may be this one: No matter what anyone tells you, the majority of people in this world do *not* appreciate being on the receiving end of a rather fragile concept known as "constructive" criticism.

Even the best-intentioned criticism is like fine wine: It does not travel well. By the time the critical comment reaches the recipient's ears, its essence has deteriorated considerably.

Example: Last week a colleague of mine — a women both intelligent and civilized — asked me a question: "Tell me, honestly," she implored. "What do you really think of my new haircut?"

On background, I will tell you in all candor that my friend's haircut was a disaster. Perpetrated upon her by someone named Mr. Bruno, it was a lopsided, short-in-the-back, long-on-the-sides affair, which made her look like a bloodhound with unusually long ears.

So I hesitated. What could I possibly say to her that would be perceived as *constructive* criticism and not its evil twin — plain, old, everyday, *destructive* criticism?

"Oh, please," my friend begged. "You know I trust your opinion and that I welcome constructive criticism."

Once again — will I never learn? — I fell into the trap.

Emboldened by her professed trust in me, I gently said it was not, in my opinion, the most becoming haircut she'd ever had. But then again, perhaps *I* just needed to get used to it.

That was about as constructive as I could get.

A silence ensued; one with a lot of things going on in it.

"Well, it may be a bit avant-garde," said my friend in a voice shot through with sarcasm, "but what's wrong with that? We can't all be frozen in the 1960s, can we?"

No. And apparently we can't all accept the fact that while there may be such a thing as constructive criticism, there is no such thing as constructive *listening* to constructive criticism.

Writer Elizabeth Bishop understood this all too well, as evidenced by her explanation of why she steadfastly refused to write criticism: "It is better, given the choice, to have friends," she pointed out.

And, I might add, given the choice, it is better to be on speaking terms with family members who, like friends, are always asking for your opinion on some thing or another.

"Mom," one of my sons used to ask — before adolescence set in and rendered him incapable of asking anyone over the age of 19 anything — "Mom, does this shirt go with these pants?"

Me: "Well, yes, dear. They look quite nice together. The Hawaiian shirt, though, might look even better with pants that aren't quite so ... so plaid."

Son: "Why don't you just come out and say I'm ugly. I'm never going out again. You think you always look so perfect."

Me: (*A long sigh. Followed by silence.*)

Some people, legend has it, respond well to criticism. I am not one of them. Which is unfortunate since I am in a profession — writing — that is the perfect setup for attracting unsolicited criticism. From readers. From family and friends. From editors. From the butcher at my super-market.

I have no defense for my inability to be cheerful when criticized, to respond, for instance: "Oh, yes! You are so right about my being wrong in that paragraph about Ming vases! And why didn't I think of bringing in — tangentially of course — the history of all the Chinese dynasties, relating it, naturally, to Ming-ware and how it foreshadowed the advent of Tupperware."

As usual, the Greeks had a word for it, for our inability to see ourselves the way others see us; i.e., in a critical light. Actually, it's more a sentence than a word; but it's a short — and amazingly insightful — sentence.

Way back in the 6th century — B.C., I believe — the Greek philosopher Xenophanes said this about the universality of self-deception:

179

"If horses could paint, they would draw gods that looked like horses."

So. We see what we want to see. We hear what we want to hear. And he who deals in criticism walks in quicksand. (I made that last bit up.)

One last thought: Should you decide to respond to this column, remember, if you can't write something nice, don't write anything at all.   ⊕

Worrying

The other day, while waiting in the checkout line at the super-market, a man I didn't know told me I looked worried.

"Cheer up," he said, smiling a cryptic little smile. "Life can't be all that bad."

I worried about his remark all the way home. His observation that I looked worried was bad news. Among other things, it implied I'd better step up the old visits to the Worriers Anonymous group where I thought I had been making progress. Now I'm worried that I was deluding myself about the progress thing.

For years, people have told me I worry too much. "Lighten up!" they'd tell me. "This savings and loan thing won't last forever!" Or they'd say: "Stop worrying about the deficit. Like, you've never had a check bounce?" And once, when I was worried dizzy that the trade balance between us and other countries was not working in our favor, friends talked me down by reminding me of the supremacy of American ham-burgers around the world.

But it would be unfair to blame my compulsive worrying entirely on the troublesome geopolitical situation.

Even as a child, I spent a lot of time worrying. I worried, for instance, that I'd lose my skate key and have to wear roller skates everywhere. Forever. And I worried a lot about catching a cold from talking on a public pay phone. Especially after the rumor spread on the block that old Mr. Huey had died from a cold picked up while talking on a public pay phone at Grand Central Station in New York City.

And the year I was 11, I worried a lot that I would grow up to be flat-chested like my Aunt Margaret. It was said to run in families.

Suffice it to say: When it comes to worrying, I've paid my dues.

I know I've got to stop worrying, but it's hard. Still, I keep trying. Last Sunday, for instance, I sat in my kitchen trying to pretend I wasn't worried about anything. But just when I thought I was getting the hang of it, my old Mickey Rooney Worry came back. With a vengeance.

Simply put, I worry about the mathematical probability that eventually I might have to marry Mickey Rooney. I figure it's just a matter of time before the much-married Mr. Rooney — now on wife No. 8 or 9 — gets around to me. I have all the necessary qualifications: I'm single, over 18, and like short men. Think about it. How many women are left out there who have those qualifications and haven't already been a Mrs. Rooney?

Still, my counselor at Worriers Anonymous tells me that it's a step in the right direction — to go from worrying about Saddam Hussein to worrying about Mickey Rooney. Simplify, simplify, simplify your worries, she keeps telling me.

I passed on this advice to some friends the other night as we sat around drinking cappuccino and discussing our worries.

"I worry about 'Seinfeld,'" said one friend. "I'm worried that Jerry might decide to move to L.A. Then where would George and Elaine and Kramer hang out?"

"Big deal," said someone else. "I'm worried that some hip, Hollywood producer will make a movie of the Nancy Drew books and cast Cher in the starring role."

I hadn't planned to contribute but, swept up in the passion of the moment, I blurted out that I was worried about how the designated hitter rule is affecting baseball.

A friend who stayed behind after the others left later confided her worry — that people found her boring. "I didn't think I was boring from first through fourth grades," she said, "but then from fourth through seventh, I thought I was. Then in the eighth and ninth grades, I wasn't again. But in 10th grade ..."

ZZZZZZZZZZZZZZZZZZZZ.

Oops. I must have dozed off there. Anyway, you get the picture. There is no end to the infinite varieties of worrying. Let me count the ways.

Or rather, let a colleague of mine — a gorgeous (she insisted I describe her that way), sharp, seasoned, perceptive newspaper reporter — count the ways:

"I worry that Mr. Right, or Mr. Half-Right, will say he can see me only one time in the next three months and it will be the day that my permanent gets frizzy; that my car won't start in the winter; that Jack the Ripper will grab me as I'm trying to unlock my front door; and mostly that I will succumb to tubs of ice cream and an entire Sara Lee cheesecake one lost weekend and emerge from my house Monday morning weighing 295 pounds, with cake crumbs still stuck on my chin."

Of course, some of her worries are just plain silly. Everyone knows Jack the Ripper's been dead for over a hundred years. ⊕

Cats

Cats, I have often observed, could teach most of us a thing or two **183** about self-esteem.

Unlike people, cats do not need or seek outside approval in order to feel good about themselves. Cats already feel good about themselves.

That is why cats — unlike dogs, for instance — do not respond to praise or try to please us by learning dopey cat tricks. Cats already have earned the only approval they need: self-approval.

I thought about all this — cats, self-esteem, stupid pet tricks and the like — last week while watching "Late Night with David Letterman" with my own cats, Max and Fluffy.

It was the night Dave — as I like to call him — had on a pet therapist named Warren Eckstein who wrote a book called "How to Get Your Cat to Do What You Want." Now, far be it for me to question Warren — as I like to call him — or his credentials, but frankly, anyone who ...

Excuse me a second.

I'm warning you for the last time, Max. MY NEW SLUBBED SILK BEDROOM CHAIR IS NOT YOUR SCRATCHING POST!

Let's see. Where were we? Oh, yes. Anyone who is owned by a cat knows that the title of Warren's book should not be "How to Get Your Cat to Do What You Want," but "How Your Cat Gets You to Do What It Wants."

I mean, get this: Warren says that to dissuade a cat from scratching, say, a slubbed silk bedroom chair, all you have to do is tape balloons to the chair. When the cat inevitably bursts a balloon, the sound will act as aversion therapy, scaring the cat into avoiding the chair.

Pardon me a sec.

OK, Fluffy, that's it. If you don't get out of my lingerie drawer and take that catnip mouse with you, I'M TAKING YOU TO THE VET!

But getting back to aversion therapy, I once had a cunning, orange-striped tabby named Harpo who developed a fondness for stalking and attacking expensive, crystal wine glasses. After breaking them, he liked to lap up a good Chardonnay or a saucy little Beaujolais. Which meant giving small, elegant dinner parties was hell. Unless, of course, you liked crushed glass in your cheese dip.

Well, I was about five years ahead of Warren in using the old aversion theory technique. To break Harpo of his cat-astrophic behavior, I started buying really cheap wine — *and not letting it breathe before serving it!* — thinking that once Harpo lapped up a truly awful Chianti he'd quit such antics. How was I to know this was a cat with a completely undiscriminating palate?

Excusez-moi.

You are walking a fine line now, Max! Get away from that Steuben vase. RIGHT NOW!

Of course, coping with a sick or injured cat presents the greatest challenge of them all. I mean, as one of the worst things you'll ever have to do, giving a cat medicine rates right up there with trying to get them into doll's clothing.

I can't tell you how often I've ground a tiny pill into fine powder, carefully sprinkled it through a pound of all-white albacore tuna, and placed it before a cat — only to have him take one short whiff and walk away.

One moment, por favor.

Drop that Rolex watch, Fluffy!

Anyway, getting back to the sick cat, liquid medicine is a bit easier to administer than pills. But the process takes three people: One to wrap the cat tightly in a towel and hold him; a second to immobilize the cat's head and jaws; and a third to slip the eyedropper of medicine into the little space between the cat's side teeth.

Oh, yes. A word about the proper attire when giving a cat medicine. Here's what I wear: An old terry-cloth bathrobe, knee socks, gloves of fine wool (mittens are no good), and a towel wrapped around my head. Of course, you can substitute as needed.

All right! That's it. Both of you! OUT OF THE HOUSE! Shredding my Barry Manilow tapes is the last straw!

By the way, did I tell you that Warren (the pet therapist, remember?) suggests you get down on the floor with your cat so you can see life as kitty sees it?

Well, I kind of took that suggestion to heart, but put my own twist on it: Instead of getting down on the floor with Max, I carried him around the house and showed him what life looks like to me. He seemed particularly interested in the top shelves in the pantry and the storage area over the kitchen sink where I keep my best china.

Which reminds me. I've got to call the plumber tomorrow about removing the Wedgewood tea cup from the kitchen disposal. ⊕

Now and Then

All time can be divided roughly into two parts: Now and the Time Before Now. And, generally speaking, people usually prefer one or the other.

A lot of people I know are enthusiastic about Now. I, however, am leaning in the direction of the Time Before Now. For one thing, it seemed a simpler time. Not complex and confusing in the way that Now is.

And for another, it was a time that didn't require so much caution and second-guessing about ordinary events in one's daily life.

The problem I have with Now is its rapidly escalating list of things one can no longer do.

Here, for example, are some notes from my journal about things I didn't do last week.

Thursday: Am still kicking myself about today's perfume faux pas. How was I to know that wearing perfume to the office is a form of female sexual harassment toward male co-workers? But there it was, printed in an article some anonymous person had placed on my desk.

No fragrance, it said. Too sexy. Don't do it. Spent most of the day hiding in the ladies' room reading magazines and wondering if it's still OK to use soap.

Magazines didn't lift my spirits. Saw article on "The New Feminists" and found myself worrying about what happened to the Old Feminists. Could their disappearance be linked to some infraction of the perfume law? And if so, does this make them victims? Remembered reading recently about a man who tried to suffocate his wife and then pleaded he was a victim of "midlife crisis." Scary.

Friday: Almost had a fatal accident driving to work this morning. Averted it just in time. Was about to roll down my car window and shout "You jerk!" to guy who'd been tailgating me, but caught myself. Keep forgetting the days are over when you can engage in friendly criticism of your fellow commuters. Unless, that is, you don't mind risking your life.

Decided instead to write a column about it. Maybe touch on the decline of civilization, blah, blah, blah. How we've returned to the wild west, blah, blah, blah. Perhaps work in some statistics on guns, violence, etc. etc. etc. Was thinking of calling it: Now and The Time Before Now.

On second thought, decided it's too risky to write such a piece. Man I almost yelled at got a look at me and knows the car I drive. Sad. But that's Now for you.

Saturday: Awakened looking forward to a leisurely cup of coffee and a slice of sour cream coffee cake. Then remembered reports that coffee thins your bones and that sour cream coffee cake fattens your thighs. Decided that while that might be a good look for some women, it could be unattractive on me. Downed a glass of carrot juice instead, followed by a bag of low-fat Cheetos.

Drove to mailbox — walking is no longer safe — to post subscription to new magazine. It's called "Nuthouse" and is described as a periodical devoted to "aggressive humor therapy." Figured aggressive humor might help me work out repressed anger about previous day's near-catastrophic tailgating incident.

Wanted to stop at bank's ATM machine to withdraw money, but

187

decided it was too risky. Wondered if ticket-seller at movie house would accept check. Then remembered where movie house is located and decided to stay home instead.

Sunday: Awakened from a dream in which I had answered a personals ad, one I'd actually seen in *Harper's* magazine. It read: "Clint Eastwood look-alike seeks bosomy woman under 30 who wants to explore her mind, soul and planet." Worried this is a sign I'm becoming too desperate. It's a totally inappropriate match.

I mean, why would I want to explore this planet? I don't even like it.

Dressed and set out for bookstore with one clear objective in mind: To buy a book.

Spirits sank at bookstore when I saw section after section of books devoted to the following "isms": appearanceism, speciesism, sizeism, biodegradeableism, ageism, New Ageism, self-helpism, vegetarianism, existentialism, deconstructionism, ethnocentrism, self-centrism, and Martha Stewartism.

Found myself in section on "non-fiction novels," where I fell into despairism.

Ended up buying a copy of "Listening to Prozac." Later read that more than six million Americans now use that anti-depressant drug. Driving home, this piece of news so depressed me that I regressed to a state of Time Before Now. Found myself suddenly at a restaurant in Little Italy ordering a double espresso and rum cake.

It seemed like old times.   ⊕

Canceled Checks

Excuse my haste, but I have to write this fairly fast. That's because

I'm due at the tax accountant's office before noon to turn over records for my income tax returns.

I know what you're thinking. That I'm disorganized. A procrastinator. Someone who puts off things until the absolute last minute. In other words, the kind of person who makes you feel quite superior and extremely good about yourself.

Look, that's OK with me. As long as you don't get it in your head to write me to say how you did your tax returns early this year or how you already used your refund check to pay for the new kitchen floor and how, if I had been more on the ball, I wouldn't be facing this deadline right now and could pay more attention to this column.

Well, I apologize for any inconvenience caused by my tardiness but, frankly, I'm just not the sort of person who enjoys reliving my life by sorting through a year's worth of canceled checks.

It was bad enough, in my opinion, to live through the incident that prompted Check No. 813 to Marty's 24-hour Emergency Locksmith

Service the night it actually happened. But to have to live through it twice — especially the part about explaining to the police at 2 a.m. why I was wearing a cowgirl outfit and how the cat got his head stuck in the broken window glass — seems downright cruel.

But, heck, Check No. 813 is the least of it. What about Check No. 646? Made out to a local travel agency, the very sight of it conjures up the memory of how ridiculous I looked in the lime green polyester shorts and Elvis sweat shirt I had to buy when my luggage never arrived in Memphis.

The Good. The Bad. The Ugly. The Humiliating. It's all there in the little piles of checks neatly arranged in the center of my bedroom floor: the story of my life in 1990. And while such a filing plan may look disorganized to the casual viewer, each pile, in fact, represents a category.

For example, Check No. 777 — made out to Madame Petroska Inc. — originally went into the category marked Personal Growth. But upon reflection, I decided the check — which covered a series of facial rejuvenation sessions with Madame — should be moved into the Wishful Thinking category.

Other checks placed into the Wishful Thinking category were No. 712 for a size 8 black leather skirt ordered from Victoria's Secret and No. 700 for a self-help tape called "How to Live Successfully With a Cat."

Man Troubles is another category requiring some thoughtful choices. Should the check for $250 worth of lingerie go into Man Troubles? Or No Regrets? I could even make a good case, I believe, for putting it into Tuition & Education since I learned more about life by hanging out at Frederick's of Hollywood than I ever did in college psychology courses.

A check for a three-month supply of a powdered diet supplement goes right into the Turning Over a New Leaf category. But then so does my check for a BackSaver's garden rake.

Which brings me to the rather large category of Back Troubles. Of course, you'll find the usual items in this category:

Check No. 722 for appliance repair (trying to load up a dishwasher by dropping the dishes into those little slots because you can't bend over,

I've found, may cause motor malfunction) and Check No. 723 for emergency carpentry services to extract a cat from the crawl space in the attic which is where he ran when he cleverly realized I couldn't bend over fast enough to stop him.

Upstairs, Downstairs: Check No. 756 for termite inspection of basement could go into this category. Or it could go into Missed Opportunities since termite inspector asked me out to dinner and I didn't go.

Missed Opportunities category could conceivably be the right spot also for Check No. 808 — which was the air fare for my vacation to Phoenix, Ariz. The flight was overbooked and anyone willing to go to Easton, Pa., instead of Phoenix got a $100 rebate on the ticket. I turned that one down, too.

All in all, I'd say that while 1990 was a good year, it was not a great year. However, I have taken steps to ensure that fiscal year 1991 is not only a great year but a vintage year. My plan? Write out only checks that fall into the Good Times or No Regrets categories.

The rest gets paid in cash. ⊕

191

Perfectionists

There are women in this world whose stockings never run. Whose lipstick never smudges. Whose flawless outfits always look as if they'd been put together by Armani or Chanel.

Diane Sawyer is one such woman.

And there are men in the world whose shirts are always crisp. Whose skin is always tan. Whose fingernails are always buffed to a shine.

Cary Grant was one such man.

And, yes, there is the occasional child whose shoelaces are always tied. Whose sweater is always buttoned correctly. Whose room is always neat.

Margaret Thatcher, I am told, was such a child.

I am speaking here of those we call "perfectionists." People who, for reasons usually known only to their parents and their psychotherapists, believe that the pursuit of flawless excellence — *in all things* — is life's highest calling.

I, on the other hand, believe that perfectionists exist among us as a reminder that a good thing can indeed be carried too far.

Case in point: I have a cousin — a notorious perfectionist — who is known to choose pets on the basis of whether their size and color clash with her home's decor. The dogs in her household have ranged from sleek greyhounds during her high-tech, Le Corbusier period, to spotted Dalmatians during her many-patterned English country period.

Fortunately, for those wishing to avoid perfectionists, it is fairly easy to spot them. Often they are attracted to such fields as orthopedic surgery, experimental physics, accounting, baseball and show business.

On the other hand, you seldom find them in football, automotive engineering or politics — unless you count dictators as politicians.

Actually, if there were such a thing as a perfectionist's resume, it would read something like this:

Dropped out of finger-painting class in nursery school to take up basic calligraphy.

By age six had mastered sophisticated combinations of color coordination — including the always tricky navy-blue-with-green pairing.

At age eight reorganized every bookshelf in house into alphabetized subject-matter categories.

Was voted "Most Polite Student and Best Dresser" three years in a row between sixth and ninth grades.

But even without seeing a resume, many perfectionists are easy to spot. Two possible tip-offs to the perfectionist woman are: Straight, blunt-cut hair and well-manicured fingernails.

Perfectionist men often favor ties knotted in the Windsor style and tattersall vests.

And it goes without saying that a perfectionist of either gender would never wear broken eyeglasses held together at the sides with tape.

(A word of caution, however: Although I admit it is paradoxical, people who cover their sofas with clear plastic are not — repeat, *not* — perfectionists.)

Personality-wise, I have found perfectionists to be impatient people. Since they know the right way to do everything, it annoys them to see it done the wrong way — which is to say, any way other than theirs.

And perfectionists, as a rule, have no empathy. They are unable to put themselves in someone else's shoes unless those shoes are perfectly polished and classically timeless in design.

Humor, also, is in short supply in perfectionist people. When, for instance, was the last time you saw Nancy Reagan doubled-up from laughing?

Which brings us to Famous Perfectionists. Here is a list of some I suspect — but can't prove — are perfectionists: Martha Stewart, George F. Will, Nancy Reagan, Barbra Streisand, Morris the Finicky Cat.

In my lifetime, I have lived with perfectionists and witnessed first-hand the addictive nature of such a pursuit. To the perfectionist, the more perfect you become, the more perfection you need so as to stay on an even keel. I once observed, for instance, how the dusting of a bathroom shelf by a perfectionist friend led to washing the wall behind it, which led to repapering the bathroom, which led to putting down a new floor.

Once, a long time ago, while trimming a hedge, I experienced the urge to perfection. After five straight hours of clipping, the hedge was perfectly groomed, each leaf folded elegantly into its rounded shape. It also had shrunk from a four-foot hedge to one that was about 14 inches high.

Since then, I take a nap whenever I sense I'm entering the danger zone of perfection. The urge is always gone when I wake up. ⊕

A Pain in the Back

My weekend of the bad back begins not with a whimper but
a bang:

Saturday — I wake up, startled by loud noise outside bedroom window. I jump up, rush to window, find I have shrunk three feet overnight
and can't see over window ledge to street below.

This discovery is followed by three important insights: One, I can't
stand up straight; two, someone during the night has inserted a number
of long, sharp knives into the lumbar region of my back; and, three, my
cats, Max and Fluffy — reverting to primitive instincts — sense my help-
lessness and move in for the kill, heading right for my Lalique crystal collection.

Decide only thing to do is distract Max and Fluffy with food. But
how to get downstairs, and, once down, how to bend over to fill their
dishes? Manage to get to kitchen, where I am visited with another
important insight: Sliding down banister is not as much fun as I remembered.

Solve problem of filling cat bowls — rather brilliantly, I think — by simply standing above cats and pouring dry cat food from boxes into two piles on kitchen floor. Max and Fluffy are ecstatic, running through cat food raining down on them, their little faces upturned to catch as much Meow Mix as possible before it hits the floor.

One problem, though: Hadn't thought about how to clean up mess afterward. Can't bend down to plug in vacuum cleaner or sweep up. Worry rest of day that I might die and that after firemen break into house, my obituary will read: "Cat Woman Found Dead in House Littered with Meow Mix."

Medicate myself with two double-strength pain killers, a muscle relaxant, a Coors Lite Beer, and an ice pack placed on back. Try to watch public TV but am in no shape to make tough, critical choice between show called "Cats and Dogs: Maintenance of Litter Boxes; Differences Between Collies and Shelties;" or "The Firing Line," which features Lester Thurow and William F. Buckley Jr. discussing economics.

Walk around house or lie on floor for next four hours. Decide to eat something but can't reach anything in cabinets except pickled beets. Spirits soar, though, when mail arrives along with a sample box of Raisin Nut Bran cereal. Eat it out of box, standing over sink. Discover that milk poured into cardboard box tastes funny.

Go to bed at 6 p.m. determined not to spend the night worrying about how Max and Fluffy seem to be having territorial fights over who gets to use the new living room sofa as a scratching post.

Sunday — Wake up from dream that Saddam Hussein is residing in my living room, which has been redecorated with sofas shaped like huge cats. Gingerly test my back. Ouch! Get up. Decide to dress and go to convenience store for necessary supplies: ice cream, peanut butter, fudge brownies, *National Enquirer,* etc., etc. Manage to get into front-zipped dress by throwing it on floor, then lying on top of it and zipping it up.

Shoes present a problem. Can't bend over to select appropriate pair. Spy high-heeled black pumps on floor, the ones I'd so wantonly kicked off on Friday night, and slip into them. Have a sudden insight: To avoid back attacks, one should probably never kick off high-heeled pumps the way chorus girls do in old, bad movies.

Catch glimpse of myself in mirror on way to bathroom and decide that my crawl-walk gait has dramatically affected the way my clothes fit. But surprised at how good pumps look when worn with red knee-hi socks.

Trip to store a disappointment. Discover I can purchase items displayed only at elbow-level height. Scrap plans for peanut butter (at floor level), fudge brownies (overhead rack) and ice cream (freezer door impossibly heavy to open) and return home with such items as Knorr's Fish Flavored Bouillon, sauerkraut juice, canned succotash, Kipper Snax, and jumbo jar of Old El Paso Refried Beans.

At home, I am hit with a deep insight and decide to work on incorporating into my novel the new angle of a woman who comes home from the opera one night, kicks off her high-heeled, black pumps and wakes up an invalid the next morning. Make some notes about metaphors and similes that could be used to demonstrate how we are all at risk, how none of us knows what the future holds. Came up with good stuff about "walking a mile in the other guy's pumps," etc., etc.

Think about calling the son who's studying Buddhism in Japan and sharing insights with him. Decide instead to break up cat fight in kitchen sink, have another Coors, kick off pumps, and go to bed. ⊕

197

Martha Stewart and Me

Women, I have observed, fall into two main categories: Those who are Martha Stewart and those who are not.

I, after a long period of denial, am resigned to being part of the latter group.

In other words: It's over. I give up. Uncle!

Or to be completely non-sexist about it: Uncle! *and* Aunt!

What can I tell you?

I tried raising my own free-range chickens. I tried making curtains from bedsheets. I tried creating centerpieces from gourds and Gouda. I tried garnishing desserts with apple-tree branches — from my own orchard — dipped in chocolate.

I tried all this. And I failed.

So I give up.

I am not proud of giving up. In fact, giving up my aspirations to Martha Stewartism is almost as painful as giving up my quest, a few years ago, for Diane Sawyerism.

(And, no, despite some rumors to the contrary, I do not believe

Martha Stewart and Diane Sawyer are actually the same person.
Although, come to think of it, I've never seen them together.)

What really finished me off — Martha Stewartism-wise — was a
recent newspaper report listing the "10 Things That Drive Martha
Stewart Crazy."

It made me realize that many of the things that drive Martha crazy
are precisely the things I could not give up.

Case in point: Unsolicited (is there any other kind?) junk mail.
Martha hates it.

I, on the other hand, look forward to these dispatches from the world
of commerce and community.

First of all, you can count on junk mail. It is one of life's constants.
Friends and family may forget to drop you a line, but junk mailers never
do.

And now that junk mail so closely resembles "unjunk" mail — often
masquerading as telegrams, invitations, checks made out to you for
$10,000, etc. — the challenge of telling one from another often makes
my day.

Secondly, and most important, junk mail is never a bill.

Martha Stewart also hates wastefulness in the home. "People should-
n't use paper towels to clean everything," she told the *Palm Beach Post*.
"Use damp rags and rinse them out."

Obviously, the Divine Miss S. has no children.

In homes where children have taken up residence, paper towels are
king.

My sons, for instance, thought nothing of going through three rolls
of paper towels per day, and four or five jumbo-sized rolls if the day
included washing the dog.

Or the car.

And any damp rags in our house were usually being worn by the
sons who, in what seems a genetically determined trait, were incapable of
waiting for the clothes dryer to finish its cycle.

In a related pet peeve, Martha Stewart declares war on dirty windows. "Just wipe them off whenever you see a spot on them," she advises.

As someone whose windows are way past the professional window-washing stage and headed for the sand-blasting option, I must demur. Clearly, Martha is unaware of — or perversely chooses to ignore — the Domino Theory of Good Housekeeping.

Which is: Clean windows let in more light. More light shows up any cleaning short-cuts taken by the less-than-perfect housekeeper.

Particularly unflattering in the clear light of day are accumulated dustballs, hairballs, and chewed-up balls of any sort thrown to amuse a cat or dog.

Ms. Martha also puts her Bass Weejun-clad foot down when it comes to "kitchen sloppiness that leads to appliance breakdown."

Whew! This is a biggie. Martha says that you ought to be able to get at least 40 years out of kitchen appliances.

I say: The only thing in my kitchen that is at least 40 years old is me.

By the way, did I mention that when Martha Stewart cut her hair short, I did too?

Although come to think of it, maybe that was when Diane Sawyer cut her hair short.

Or did I mention that when Martha Stewart baked a cake for 80 at her Barnard College reunion, I had three friends over for coffee and a Pillsbury marble-mix cake?

But, hey, enough already.

On the other hand, if you want more, I'd suggest you pick up a copy of my new magazine: *All About Martha Stewart and Me.*　⊕·

ALICE STEINBACH

Role Models

201

At least once a year, some magazine or another will put together and publish a list of the "Ten People We Most Admire." Inevitably the selections are: the President and First Lady; former Presidents and First Ladies; celebrities such as Oprah Winfrey; a retired military person like Colin Powell (it always helps to have a best-selling book); and, of course, Mother Teresa.

But I suspect that most of us, if asked to draw up a personal list of role models, would include none of the above. A real role model, it seems to me, is someone who influences our view of the world in ways that count: through love, through teaching, through living example. It is the kind of influence that lasts a lifetime, constantly shaping and reshaping our attitudes.

And although we tend to think that role models are necessary only in our youth, I believe it's never too late to add a new name to our list. In fact, as we grow older, the possibilities widen. Maturity can act like a magnifying glass when it comes to spotting true value in another person: what might have passed unnoticed in one's more callow days is suddenly rendered with great clarity.

It's also thought that role models must be of a certain, advanced age. I disagree. Increasingly, I admire the courage of young people and, for that reason, have here included celebrations of two adolescent girls — one known to the world, the other unknown. In my way of thinking, and in my life, they easily qualify as role models.

Lessons from a Wise Fox

E very year at about this time, when the air turns sharp and the sun begins its slow ascent into higher skies, I think about my mother, about the way she was always the first to point out the early signs of autumn: the evening sky marbled with streaks of smoke from a neighbor's fireplace; the sudden urgency of the sparrow's song; the pale, thinned-out morning light that foreshadows winter.

My mother's birthday was in October — as mine is — and when I was a child she liked to say that the fates had smiled on us, that we were exceptionally lucky to be born in a month so full of change but at the same time so temperate and predictable.

"You can go almost anywhere in the world in October," she would say, "and the weather will be near perfect." Then she'd go on to say there were lessons to be learned from nature in the fall. And she'd make up a fable in which a talking fox would give voice to the idea that change is not just an ending but a beginning as well.

"You must remember," the wise fox would always say at the end, "that the leaves which die in the fall are born again in the spring."

Balance and counter-balance; harmony and disharmony; loss and renewal; they seemed to be the themes that ran through my mother's lifelong search for order and meaning in the world. And in herself.

A memory: When I was seven, on the night of my mother's 40th birthday, she took me outside to stand beneath a moon so bright it lit up every corner of the garden. "Look at the moon through these," my mother said, handing me the binoculars given to her as a birthday gift. "You see that reddish area? That's the Sea of Tranquility. And the blue shadow to its side? That's called the Ocean of Storms." Then she said something about how in life it was necessary to learn to navigate both.

But to be honest, standing in the garden with my mother on the night of her 40th birthday, I didn't see either the Sea of Tranquility or the Ocean of Storms. Staring through the binoculars at the moon, dizzy with contentment, I saw only my mother's face swimming above me through pale stars in a dark blue sky.

I thought about all this last week as I stood drinking coffee in my own garden in the cool, hickory-scented evening air. I watched the moon appear and disappear as it worked its way through the delicate tracery of trees outlined on the horizon. And suddenly I found myself thinking that my mother would have fashioned a fable from such material. The thought of what the fox might say made me smile.

And before I knew it, I was zipping down a road into the past, traveling through happy, funny, sometimes zany memories that had to do with my mother. Like the time she let me drive the family Plymouth a mile or so down the backroads from my stepfather's farmhouse to the combination gas station-grocery store. I was 11 at the time and we wound up — my mother, brother, the family dog and me — unhurt in a neighbor's cornfield.

The memory of that day made me laugh out loud. And it was then I realized that this was the first time in the five years since her death that I had thought of my mother without deep feelings of sadness and loss. Frankly, I had begun to think I would never make my peace with her death. And even though I realize the experience of grief has no set timetable for everyone, the length and depth of my feelings had become somewhat embarrassing to me. Mainly, I kept them to myself.

So it was with great relief that I welcomed back from exile these happy memories of my mother. Their return emboldened me to open other closed doors.

And so I sat the other night on the floor of my room holding my mother's handbag. I had brought it home with me from the hospital on the day of her death, but in the five intervening years had not been able to open it. It reminded me too much of the profound truth I wanted to forget: I was never going to see my mother again. Never.

Here is what I found along with the lipstick and wallet and photos of her grandchildren: A folded piece of paper upon which my mother, in her elegant penmanship, had written down these lines from Wendell Berry, one of her favorite nature writers:

"Always in the big woods, when you leave familiar ground and step off alone into a new place, there will be, along with the feelings of curiosity and excitement, a little nagging of dread. It is the ancient fear of the unknown, and it is your first bond with the wilderness you are going into."

My mother. Still teaching after all these years. ⊕

Well, Here We Are

I come from a family that never planned summer vacations. As a child, I would just wake up one morning and find the curtains closed in every room of the house, the car loaded up with suitcases, and my father standing above my bed saying, "let's go!"

At least that's the way I remember it: childhood vacations as spontaneous and full of surprises as life itself.

Usually there were five of us in the car: my parents, grandmother, older brother, and me. Occasionally, out of pity, a stray cousin or an unmarried aunt got invited along and, after the inevitable fight about who got to sit next to the window, we would head to the backroads and the so-called "scenic" route.

Early morning departures were de rigueur: Dawn would be breaking — lavender and gray slants of light filtering down through the sparkling, early morning dew — as we pulled out of the garage and headed up the alley behind our house. I was barely awake; often I slept for the first hundred miles or so, my head resting on my grandmother's shoulder.

We never knew exactly where we were headed, although usually, to escape the summer heat, it would be some place north like New England or upstate New York. My father was in charge of driving and destinations, and he didn't like to talk much about either.

He was a traveling man by profession, my father; accustomed to the pressures of having to be, for example, in Brazil on precisely a given date. Or India. Or you-name-it. What he needed from a vacation, he liked to say, was a sense of leisure, of unstructured time that did not require a calendar or a clock or being at such-and-such a place at such-and-such a time.

That was what the word "vacation" meant to him, he said: a vacation was not a *place* but a state of mind.

And although I could not have articulated it then, there was something else I recognized, even as a child, about my father's approach not only to vacations but to everything else as well: He was a man who, in his short life, was more interested in the journey than the destination, enjoying each mile of the trip for what it was and not where it ended.

It didn't seem to bother him, for instance, that my brother, cousin, and I bickered and fought with regularity during the trip. Or that my mother regularly threatened to stop the car right on the highway, put the three of us out, and make us walk back to Baltimore. Each morning my father emerged refreshed from whatever guest cottage we had stopped at, eager to resume the trip.

And so it was in the summer of my eighth year that we found ourselves in Massachusetts — car windows rolled down, hot, dusty breezes blowing in the left window and out the right — studying a white sign shaped like an arrow and neatly lettered: MOHAWK TRAIL. It pointed to the left.

"Well, here we are," my father said, heading left. It's what he always said when some decision or another had been reached by him: Well, here we are. And although I had no idea where we were, it didn't matter: The combination of an exotic-sounding place like the Mohawk Trail, combined with my father's familiar *"Well, here we are,"* was good enough for me.

207

It was our last trip together — the next year my father was killed — and for years I could remember very little of that vacation. Just the white sign, an arrow pointing left, and the words MOHAWK TRAIL.

Then, about five years ago, while driving from Williamstown, Mass., to Boston with a college-bound son, I saw the sign — or one just like it — again. As it turned out, we were already driving along the Mohawk Trail, so it was not a matter of consciously deciding to retrace my childhood trip.

As we drove along the winding, hilly roads, I felt disappointment; nothing looked even vaguely familiar to me — until we arrived at the combination souvenir shop and three-story lookout tower at the top of Hairpin Turn.

We stopped at the shop, my son and I, to stretch our legs and browse through the T-shirts, Indian tomahawks and beaded moccasins. The store smelled of cedar and maple syrup, and suddenly — don't ask me why — I knew I had been here before. When I was eight years old.

It was the oddest feeling: standing in a souvenir shop in the middle of nowhere, a grown woman with a college-age son, remembering in ways deeper than ordinary memory, the child who stood in the same spot many summers before.

I turned and followed my son up the steps to the lookout tower, where we silently viewed the valley spread out below us. Then, to my surprise, I heard a voice — my own — saying: *"Well, here we are."*   ⊕

The Real Me

S omewhere recently I read an article — written by a woman whose
name I can't remember — that began something like this:

I had a wonderful personality until I was about 13 years old. Then I was simply too tired to have it anymore.

I don't know how that thought strikes you, but when I read it, I breathed a sigh of relief. I knew exactly what the writer meant about the exorbitant amount of energy it takes to maintain a "wonderful" (*read: false*) personality.

Trust me on this one: Trying to be what you think everyone wants you to be — while at the same time convincing yourself this is the way you really are — can be exhausting.

I know. Because I had a wonderful personality until I was about 35 years old. Then I lost it.

Or to be more precise, it lost me.

Up to that point, I had been quite successful in my approach to "developing" my personality: I simply patterned (*read: imitated*) most of my responses after those I observed in the people I admired.

It was a trick I learned from my Aunt Claire, who counseled me on the question of acquiring style and originality. Her advice, as I recall, went something like this: "It's not difficult to be an original. You just find someone you admire and then you copy everything about them."

In grade school, my role model was Constance Coleman, the smartest, most popular girl in my class. I worked very hard to be just like her — even though she left me in the dust in every department: brains, looks, and her incomparable talent as a tap dancer.

In junior high school, I tried to react to everything the way I imagined Miss Dennis, my favorite teacher and a most sophisticated woman, would react. (I knew Miss Dennis was sophisticated because I had seen her smoking in the teachers' lounge and she used a long, silver cigarette holder!) When, for instance, I wasn't asked to the stupid eighth-grade Halloween Hop, I simply wondered, "How would Miss Dennis handle this?"

But her influence faded when I reached high school and abandoned my emulation of anyone adult, succumbing instead to what the sociologists call peer pressure: In my crowd, we walked alike, we talked alike, we looked alike and, most important, we liked alike and disliked alike.

As I moved out of my teens and into my 20s, I worked hard at developing a personality that would be attractive to potential bosses, potential husbands, and potential mothers-in-law. I guess it worked because — and I hope you understand that this is the condensed, *Reader's Digest* version of my life — by the time I was 24, I was employed, married, and had a mother-in-law.

The next decade or so of my life was spent in search of wife-and-mother role models. I studied all my friends, I studied all *their* friends, I studied the generation ahead of me, and I read everything I could lay my hands on looking for clues as to how the perfect wife and mother got to be the perfect wife and mother.

Then, as I approached the age of 35, I inexplicably — but not unexpectedly — found myself having some difficulty finding myself. The Me that was reflected back through other people's eyes just didn't seem to cut it anymore. What I saw in this mirror of sorts wasn't a bad life; it just did-n't seem to be *my* life.

More and more, as I recall it, I found myself diving down, below the wonderful personality floating on the surface, to search for whatever truth lay beneath. Often it was touch and go, since I sometimes had to pass Miss Dennis on the way down and Constance Coleman on the way up. But gradually I found a person emerging — murky but definitely there — who seemed to be calling the shots.

At first I didn't always like this person. Nor did my family and friends. And with good reason. The New Me was less pleasant, less accommodating, and less imitative of good role models. But more real.

And whew! What a job it was! Taking all this real stuff that made up the Real Me and trying to shape it into an authentic person.

Suffice it to say: Years passed. I worked hard. I laughed. I cried. I got divorced. I got fired. I got hired. I yelled at my kids. I loved my kids. (Another *Reader's Digest* condensation. Write in for full details.)

211

And that's not The End. Here I am, still trying after all these years to pin down the elusive Real Me. But that's the funny thing about chasing after your true self: Just when you think you've caught it, it takes off again in some new direction.

Still, I'd suggest you give it a try. You might just find that living life as yourself will suit you to a "T."   ⊕

Taught by Children

O f all the pronouncements I've ever read about family life, this one is my favorite: The value of marriage is not that adults produce children, but that children produce adults.

Why am I so drawn to this observation? Because, in my case at least, it's dead on the money.

Which is to say: 20-some years ago, my children took on an undisciplined, wet-behind-the-ears candidate for adulthood and worked hard to successfully shape her into something resembling a grown-up.

And, I might add, a more interesting grown-up than she ever would have been without their unflagging input.

Here, for example, are a few of the things I've learned from my sons: Who Murray Gell-Mann is (a physicist); where Ashiya is located (outside of Osaka); what a 5.8 means to a rock climber (degree of difficulty); how to eat sea urchin (carefully); and what to do when skiing in avalanche terrain (wear your new electronic avalanche transmitter/locater.)

Were it not for my sons, I likely would know very little — if anything — about Mr. Gell-Mann or the geography of Japan or the etiquette of avalanche events.

Such topics, to be perfectly frank, do not fall naturally into my spheres of interest.

Or, to be more precise, they didn't until I had children.

Before children, my interests tended toward such things as: vacations, ambition, money, clothes, parties, and better hair.

In other words, before children, I was interested in things that had to do with: Me. Who I was. What I wanted. Where I was headed in life. What people thought of me. What *I* thought of me.

Strange, I know, but at the time it seemed a broad spectrum of interests.

Then my sons were born and I saw how narrow my line of vision had been. With their help, a new era began in my life. Call it: The Education of Me.

From my sons, I have learned more than a little about insect collecting, harmonica playing, fishing, archery, rock climbing, physics, skiing, emergency mountain rescue, purchasing a cat in Japan, how a laser works, what a first ascent is, where to find the best bar in Key West, and how to make your own backpack.

Parents, no doubt, have always learned from their children. But the world of our children seems much larger than that of previous generations, offering us even more opportunities to learn from them.

It's not unusual today for our children to work and live half-way across the world. Hardly a month goes by without bringing news that this son's friend is working in Africa or that son's classmate is living in Tibet.

A college alumni magazine features wedding photos of Rob, living now in Hong Kong, and recently married to a Chinese woman. And of Katie, living in Prague, and engaged to a Polish mathematics teacher.

The most recent issue features a picture of one of my own sons, attending the wedding in Kyoto of a classmate and a Japanese woman.

Our children lead lives we only dreamed of. The world is their stage. Though they are still in their 20s, my sons' resumes are already more interesting than mine.

They know more than I did at their age, too. And they are willing, no, eager, to teach me what they know.

And, in one of the rare instances where our needs dovetail, I am willing, no, eager, to learn from them.

Sometimes I'm surprised at just how much my sons have broadened my field of vision. In a bookstore not too long ago, I found myself buying two books: "Fear of Physics" and "Modern Japan."

In Paris last year, I found myself seeking out a physics lab I'd heard a son talk about.

And in Oxford I made a special trip to the Ashmolean Museum to see some rare Japanese prints of ancient Toyko. Which, by the way, was called Edo, not Toyko, in those days.

Because the world of our children is much larger than ours ever was, I used to worry that I was being left behind. I worried about losing touch. It took me a long time to get used to the idea that my sons and I no longer live in the same time zone.

It took even longer to deal with the idea that every time I talk to the younger son, it's already tomorrow. For him, anyway.

But then the talk starts and the ideas go back and forth and I'm asking questions and he's answering and, happily, the connection between us is stronger than ever. ⊕

Two Unusual People

Two of the world's most unusual people died recently. But unlike the widely mourned passing of two other unusual people in the same month — Dizzy Gillespie and Rudolph Nureyev — the deaths of Yvonne and Yvette McCarther early in January were scarcely noted.

"Yvonne and Yvette McCarther, Siamese twins joined at the head, have died at age 43," reported one brief wire service story. "The sisters were among the world's oldest unseparated Siamese twins.... They were found dead in their home, apparently of natural causes."

It was great talent, of course, that set Gillespie and Nureyev apart from the rest of us. And we remember and honor them for that.

What made Yvonne and Yvette so unusual was not talent but an awesome accident of birth that rendered them physically different from almost every other human being in the world. But anyone who ever met these two women would agree that they too deserve to be remembered with honor: honor for the way they managed to carve out lives of dignity despite the sometimes cruel responses to the way they looked.

I learned this about the McCarther twins firsthand when I spent two

days interviewing them. The year was 1988 and Yvonne and Yvette had
just enrolled at Compton Community College. The road to this sunny
California campus had been a winding one for the twins, with detours
that took them through stints as sideshow attractions in circuses and in
carnivals.

It's odd, but the two things that struck me first about Yvonne and
Yvette were their humor and their stylish way of dressing. I didn't expect
either.

"Hi, ladies. Love those coats," one classmate called out as he walked
by.

"Thanks, hon, but I can't stop to talk," said Yvonne. "I'm late for
class."

"Yeah, thanks," said Yvette. "But I can't stop to talk either. I'm late for
class, too."

They were also graceful. Whatever they did, their movements were
perfectly, almost eerily, synchronized. Connected at the top of their heads,
the twins had to walk with their necks tilted at almost a 90 degree angle,
a condition that prevented each from ever looking directly into the
other's eyes. To see each other, they had to look in a mirror.

With grace and humor they accepted a physical condition that
would be unthinkable to most people. "I'd rather be dead than be like
that," was the response of some who read the story.

But the twins didn't feel that way. The idea of surgical separation was
unacceptable to them. "We just never think about separation, hon," said
Yvonne. "We're happy this way," said Yvette.

Their physical condition was rare — doctors estimate such an
abnormality occurs perhaps once in every 2.5 million births — but rarer
still was the twins' attitude toward life. Against all odds, they became
outgoing, trusting human beings. And those who came to know them
eventually saw not their abnormality but two women who represented a
triumph of the human spirit.

"When you first meet them, you kind of feel sorry for them,"
Cordell McDonald, their math professor, told me. "But after you get to

know them, you kind of feel sorry for yourself. They know who they are in a way that's quite unique."

The summer before I met them, Yvonne and Yvette had worked at a summer camp for handicapped youths. They did not consider their own condition a handicap. "You can call it that if you like," said Yvonne, "but it's not a handicap" — and they were moved by the children at the camp.

"We had to be their eyes when they were blind," Yvonne said simply. "And the hands for those who couldn't use their own," added Yvette.

Although the twins had separate brains and normally developed bodies, their blood circulation was shared. And they knew that when one of them died, the other would die also. But Yvonne brushed aside the inevitable, saying: "If you can't understand that we're happy, then you just don't understand what being Siamese twins is all about."

Remembering Yvonne and Yvette, you understand what it was all about. It was about closeness. About acceptance. And, above all, about courage.   ⊕

217

17 Years, 11 Months, and 13 Days

When her family and friends talk about Kimberly Erica May, they recall a girl who knew what she wanted; a bright, curious, high-spirited girl who didn't believe in wasting time. Time, she told one of her teachers, is a priceless but perishable gift and she meant to live her life to the fullest.

And she did just that. An honor graduate of the Maryvale Preparatory School, computer whiz, basketball player, artist, choir member, recipient of the Faculty Award for school spirit and the Religion Award, Kimberly planned to enter the College of Notre Dame of Maryland this fall to study biochemistry on a partial scholarship. It was all there — an accounting of the awards, the honors, the accomplishments — in the obituary that ran last week in the pages of *The Baltimore Sun*. The brief notice was accompanied by a photograph of Kimberly, her arresting face telegraphing a rich inner life.

"She was an unusual girl, a girl who was far beyond the 17 years, 11 months and 13 days she lived," says her father, Eric May, his exact accounting of Kimberly's short life conveying a poignancy beyond words.

Of course, the death of any young person is cause for sorrow — diminishing as it does the future of us all — but it seems especially so when that person seems perched, as Kimberly was, on the doorstep of a full and giving life. And in a time when we routinely mark the passing of the famous and the celebrated, it seems important, somehow, to appreciate the life of someone like Kimberly Erica May who, in her 17 years, 11 months and 13 days, made a difference in the lives of all who knew her.

She died on Friday, Sept. 18, at 1 a.m., succumbing finally to the cancer she had fought for more than six years. Buried Sept. 22, Kimberly had planned her funeral down to the last detail. And while it was not in her power to determine the day of her death, it seems fitting that she was laid to rest on the last day of summer; that she went with the flowers, the warmth, and the brilliant light of that high, bold season.

The day after the funeral, some of her family and friends gathered together in the Mays' neat, comfortable, suburban home and, with much more joy than sorrow, remembered the girl whose presence is everywhere in the house. It is there in the paintings and drawings by Kimberly that show clear evidence of a genuine talent; in the photographs lining the walls that mark her progression from an alert-looking infant to a naturally elegant and stylish teen-ager; in the Apple computer that still contains a story she was writing; in her pink-and-white bedroom where her pet fish, Betta, still swims round and round in a crystal bowl on the vanity table.

219

But more than anything else, Kimberly's presence is evident in the people who remember her. And what emerges among the laughter and the memories and the tears is a picture of a lively, opinionated, curious, intense, creative girl, someone determined to do things her own way.

Her mother, Sharon May, says: "When Kimberly was making her funeral arrangements, she asked [the] Rev. [James D.] Hill to speak at the services. And he described her absolutely perfectly. He said she was a gentle, sweet dictator — and we all had to laugh because that was Kimberly. She felt there were certain things that had to be done and they had to be done in a certain way and they had to be done *now*."

The remark brings a smile to her grandfather's face. "This guy," says Charles Harper of his granddaughter, "was just a very determined sort of person. She was just unusually curious and she pushed and pushed and pushed to get the answer that suited the situation. That was Kim. And I admired her for it."

Who knows — perhaps she felt the push of time more keenly than most. Diagnosed at 11 as having Wilms' tumor, a kidney-related cancer, Kimberly had been through countless operations and many cycles of chemotherapy and radiation, none of which slowed her down. "Kimberly made the treatment fit around her schedule and life and the things she wanted to do," says her mother. "She would tell the doctors, 'Look, this has to fit in with class day and my trip to Europe. ...'" The mother laughs at the memory. "We feel very, very fortunate that Kimberly was able to do much of what she wanted to do."

She kept up with her studies, too, despite the hospitalizations and the nausea from the treatment and whatever else her body had to adjust to. "She would come back to school almost immediately after treatment and pick up what she had missed right away," says Sister Margaret Connor, who was Kimberly's religion teacher at Maryvale and a close friend. "And she was an excellent student. It wasn't until April that she really began not keeping the pace. ... But she was a model of courage. Courage isn't even a strong enough word."

Her brother, Eric, calls Kimberly his "second mother." He also remembers her as "always working out things scientifically. Her room was like a workshop. She was always mapping things out, and if something didn't work, it was back to the drawing board. She was sort of like a mad scientist," he says, his voice full of affection.

She was also, says her mother, a girl of "deep faith. She was Methodist. I'm Methodist, her father's Baptist, and she went to a Catholic school. She covered all the bases. But she handled the illness in her own way."

Take, for example, the Halloween costume she chose in her sopho-more year. "We worked with her on a positive attitude," says her grandmother, Charlotte Harper, as she hands you a photograph taken of Kimberly at a Halloween party that year. "This is evidence of what she did. She was bald from the treatments and she just took off her wig and polished her bare head and went as Yul Brynner in 'The King and I.'" The photograph shows a smiling Kimberly, dressed in red silk harem-type pants and a gold top, bald head shining, a perfect and, one might add, elegant evocation of the King of Siam.

Her mother laughs. "Well, you know, her attitude there was why waste a perfectly good bald head?"

It was also, says her father, Kimberly's way of letting her classmates know of her illness. She had told a few close friends, but until her sophomore year it was not generally known among the students that she had cancer. "She was a leader," says Mia Scharper, her best friend, "and every single person in the school knew her. Not because of her illness, but more through her personality and her warmth."

Kim and Mia. They met in the ninth grade and, in the special way of teen-age girls, formed an unbreakable bond. At graduation, Mia shared the religion award with Kim. Says Sister Margaret: "The whole department agreed the award had to go to Kim and Mia — not so much for the intellectual knowledge that was gained, but because the two of them traveled a journey with each other that certainly spoke of what Christian values are all about."

They were both to start college at Notre Dame. But just two weeks before she was due on campus, Kimberly had to withdraw. "That was kind of devastating for her," says her mother.

The end was drawing near. There had been six hospitalizations over the summer and, on Sept. 6, Kimberly entered the hospital for the final time. One of her last acts, says her father, was to visit a young man "who had some of the same problems she did. To tell him everything would be OK. After that day, she really didn't walk again; she just couldn't get up."

On Thursday, Sept. 10, days before she lapsed into unconsciousness and a week before her death, Kimberly called Mia. "She told me she was dying," says Mia. "She said, 'I love you. Goodbye.'"

That Thursday, apparently, was the turning point for Kimberly. She called her family in and proceeded to make her funeral plans. "Kim was aware of her condition," says her mother. "She knew she didn't have a lot of time left and she sat down with us and essentially planned her funeral herself. She told me she wanted to be buried under a tree, near some water. And she told Sister Margaret she did not want a lot to be said about what she did and who she was; instead, she had some messages she wanted delivered to people her own age and also to the adults who would be there."

Says her father: "Kim didn't want a funeral service; she wanted a celebration of her life."

One by one, they recall their last words with Kimberly.

The brother: "She asked everybody to step outside of her room so she could have a conversation with me. And she said, 'Well, Eric, Mommy told you that I'm dying and I want you to be strong. I don't want you to feel sorry for yourself when I'm gone. After I'm gone, just remember me for what I was. And what I'll always be — your sister. And I want you to remember the times we had together, both good and bad.'"

The mother: "It was Sunday morning, sometime between 5 a.m. and 7 a.m. I heard Kimberly saying to the nurse, 'I've got to relax, I've got to relax.' And the nurse was kind of at a loss. They didn't want to give her too much sleeping medication. I couldn't sleep so I got up and talked to her. I put my arm around her and rested my head on her chest. And Kimberly said to me that she was so glad I had been there for her and that I had helped her and that I had been so strong for her. ... And I remember sitting there, holding her hand. I'm not the deeply religious person that my mother is or that Kimberly was, but as I sat there I said, 'God, hold my hand, as I hold hers. Help her to relax. Let her go to sleep.' And I hadn't put the period on that thought before I realized she had gone off to sleep."

But it was the father who was at the daughter's side when the moment of death arrived. It had been the father who told the daughter to keep fighting, to "go for it," to not give up. Now he sighs — a deep, inward sigh — and says: "I was sitting there, holding her hand, and I finally leaned over and whispered in her ear, 'Baby, you don't have to fight for Daddy anymore. You're tired. It's OK to go to sleep.' I heard a terrible thunderstorm begin outside, a huge clap of thunder and, at that moment, I saw that she was gone."

Kimberly's funeral and burial took place on a bright, breezy day and went exactly as she had planned it. Everyone she loved was there. They sang the songs she had picked out and delivered the message that life is to be lived, and lived to the fullest. She was buried under a tree, near some water, a spot picked out by her mother.

She needs no epitaph, but something said by her friend, Mia, lingers in the mind and suggests, perhaps, the most appropriate way to remember Kimberly Erica May: "Every person who ever knew her has some memories of Kim laughing." ⊕

Pioneer Women

Hannah Hoisington was a young mother living on the Kansas frontier when she grabbed a revolver and an ax and spent five nights at a nearby cabin, defending a sick neighbor from packs of attacking wolves.

Amelia Stewart Knight was making a six-month overland journey to the Oregon Territory when she gave birth, by the roadside, to her eighth child. With her newborn in her arms and seven other children to care for, she crossed the Columbia River by canoe and flatboat to finally reach Oregon.

Ellen Smith was widowed on the journey to Oregon and left to travel westward with her nine children, the youngest barely two years old. When a daughter died on the trail, the frantic mother, fearing the body would be uncovered by wolves, dug the deep grave herself. Then, her provisions exhausted, she tied the smaller children to oxen and trudged on to Salem, Ore., where she and her eight children cleared the land and built a house.

Hannah Hoisington. Amelia Stewart Knight. Ellen Smith. You won't find their names in the history books, but along with thousands of other pioneer women of the 1800s they endured blizzards, droughts, Indian raids, buffalo stampedes, near-starvation, childbirth and children's deaths before reaching and settling the frontiers of the wild West.

They were ordinary women — if women of such astonishing tenacity and courage can be called ordinary — and their efforts to endure in a harsh land, through the great terrors and small triumphs of daily life, add up to a history of survival. They were wives and mothers and daughters, black women and white women. A large measure of what we admiringly define as the American character was forged on the anvil of their strength.

March is Women's History Month, and for women anxious to discover their collective past, there is a lot of catching up to be done — a lot of filling in of gaps. "Women have constituted the most spectacular casualty of traditional history," observed one well-known historian, Arthur Schlesinger Jr. "They have made up at least half the human race, but you could never tell that by looking at the books historians write."

A woman's place in history, suggested Schlesinger, is not in the textbooks.

American pioneer women wrote their own history of the westward journey: They wrote it in diaries kept while traveling the perilous Overland Trail; in letters sent home to sorely missed friends and family in the East; and in memoirs handed down to daughters and granddaughters as family records.

Here, for instance, from a collection of memoirs put together by Joanna Stratton in her book, "Pioneer Women: Voices from the Kansas Frontier," is the way Annette Lecleve remembers a day in 1873 when her "brave mother," left alone in an isolated frame house in frontier Kansas, went into early labor:

"Now that was a terrifying situation," wrote the daughter. "Alone with two babies, one four and the other 18 months, not a neighbor that could be called, no doctor to be gotten. So my brave mother got the baby clothes together on a chair by the bed, water and scissors and what else was needed to take care of the baby; drew a bucket of fresh water from a 60-foot well; made some bread-and-butter sandwiches; and set out some milk for the babies." At noon, she gave birth to a boy.

Another account of the stark realities facing women on the Overland Trail is recounted in "Women's Diaries of the Westward Journey," by Lillian Schlissel. The diary of Elizabeth Smith Geer revealed the conditions encountered in November 1847 as she, her sick husband and their seven children struggled to reach the Oregon territory:

"It rains and snows. We start this morning around the falls with our wagons. ... I carry my babe and lead, or rather carry, another through snow, mud and water, almost to my knees. It is the worst road. ... I went ahead with my children and I was afraid to look behind me for fear of seeing the wagons turn over into the mud. ... My children gave out with cold and fatigue and could not travel. ... I was so cold and numb I could not tell by feeling that I had any feet at all ... there was not one dry thread on one of us — not even my babe. ... I have not told you half we suffered. I am not adequate to the task."

Many of the women who settled in Kansas lived through and wrote about the great drought that afflicted that state from June 1859 until November 1860. In her memoir, Laura Elizabeth Belts recalled the desperate efforts of her mother, Mary Belts, to save her family from starvation during the bitter winter months while waiting for her husband to return from Iowa with food:

"How fast the scant provisions disappeared in spite of my mother's care. ... Then came a day when there was nothing to eat but the nuts and pork. My baby brother, about two years old, would not eat such food and he cried for bread, and there was none to give him. That was more than my mother could bear and she broke down and cried. It was the only time we children saw her other than brave and hopeful all through those long, trying weeks. The cold was intense, and the wind fierce, and the wolves would come and fight with our dogs right on the door stone, and how it would frighten us."

Unlike the men associated with the westward expansion — men like Wyatt Earp, John Fremont and Wild Bill Hickok, whose legends persist

— pioneer women such as Mary Belts remain, for the most part, obscure.

"There were very few heroines with a capital *H* in the story of Kansas," observed Katherine Oliver, whose own mother emigrated to Kansas in 1868 at the age of 32. "Their service was their valor; valor to 'carry on' ... in dugout or shack, in tent or room 'n' lean-to, with the same industry, persistence and cheerfulness as in the comfortable homes 'back East.'"

Usually, the decision to uproot the family and travel west was made by the men. One of every five women traveling west was pregnant, and almost every married woman traveled with small children. "Women were part of the journey because their fathers, husbands and brothers had determined to go," writes Lillian Schlissel in the introduction to her book of diaries. "The women went west because there was no way for them *not* to go once the decision was made."

The voices from the diaries tell us of the anguish and pain felt by the women forced to leave the stable, domestic existence that had formed the center of their lives. Mary A. Jones tells of her response to her husband's intentions to head for California in 1846: "I said, 'O let us not go' ... but it made no difference."

The illness or poor health of a family member was no deterrent to making the long, grinding journey: "I had never been in good health," wrote Mrs. M. S. Hockensmith before leaving for Oregon with her husband, "and there were diverse opinions as to whether I would improve or fail under the stress of the trip."

Once the journey started, it was left to the women to provide not only the semblance of a home life for their families, but also to participate in the difficult physical work required. Martha Morrison, a girl of 13 when she embarked with her family in 1844 on the trip west, made these observations about life on the trail:

"The men had a great deal of anxiety and all the care of their families, but still the mothers had the families directly in their hands and were with them all the time, especially during sickness. ...The women helped pitch the tents, helped unload, and helped yoke up the cattle. Some of the women did nearly all of the yoking: many times the men were off."

Pioneer women learned to cook in the wind and rain, to load and unload the wagons at river crossings — sometimes 2,000 pounds of supplies and possessions — and to nurse the sick with homemade medicines. They also learned to bury their children by the roadside and to move on, no matter how heavy the grief. "I remember distinctly one girl about my own age who died and was buried on the road," wrote Martha Morrison. "Her mother had a great deal of trouble and suffering. It strikes me, as I think of it now, that mothers on the road had to undergo more trial and suffering than anybody else."

Pioneer women also had to cope with the isolation of wilderness life. With the men often gone for weeks at a time and no neighbors around for companionship, each woman had to summon up her own inner resources to meet the challenge of solitude. Esther Clark recalled how her mother battled the intense loneliness of life on the Kansas prairies: "The unbroken prairies stretched for miles outside, and the wistful-faced sheep were always near at hand. Often mother used to go out and lie down among them, for company, when she was alone for the day ..."

228

In the end, the diaries, memoirs and letters written by and about these pioneering women constitute a collection of profiles in courage: individual acts of daily valor carried out far from the scrutiny and scope of historians.

"History chronicles the large and glorious deeds of the standard bearers ... and tells nothing at all of the courageous women who keep the business of the house going," wrote Lilla Day Monroe, who was the first woman admitted to practice before the Kansas Supreme Court, and who began collecting frontier reminiscences in the early 1920s.

"The world has never seen such hardihood, such perseverance, such devotion, nor such ingenuity in making the best of everything as was displayed by America's pioneer women. Their like has never been known." ⊕

Anne Frank

H ad Anne Frank lived, she would have been 60 years old today. Sixty years old! It is almost impossible to reconcile that fact with the unforgettable picture of her strong and glowing young face that is so familiar to us now.

Caught forever between childhood and adolescence in that famous and moving photograph, Anne Frank, who died at the age of 15 in a Nazi concentration camp, remains to many of us one of the most vivid and haunting examples of how strength and character and beauty of spirit can overcome even the most terrible circumstances.

The house at 263 Prinsengracht in Amsterdam, which for over two years was the hiding place for Anne and seven other Jews, is a tall, narrow, old brick building. It is no longer occupied. Its windows are now blank and empty and there are a few illegible words scrawled on the door. Inside, if you stand at the window Anne so loved (it was her only contact with the outside world), you will look into, on the right side of the garden, not 30 yards away, the back window of a house in which the French philosopher Descartes once lived. From this very house he wrote to a friend, "Is there any other country in which one can enjoy freedom as enormously as one does here?"

Anne's papers are preserved in a metal box deposited in an old, green office safe in Amsterdam. In the box lies her diary with the red, checked cover. She got the diary for her 13th birthday, just a month before she and her family went into hiding from the Nazis. Shortly after the Franks were arrested, the papers and the diary were accidentally discovered by two women who had helped them in hiding. The documents were kept in a safe for the rest of the war and then were given to Anne's father, Otto Frank, the only survivor of the eight people who had lived at 263 Prinsengracht, when he returned to Amsterdam in 1945.

Anne Frank's diary is the story of a young girl simultaneously awakening to life — and to death. Despite the grimness of her situation, most of Anne's diary deals with the preoccupations and thoughts so central to all adolescents — her relationships with her parents and sister, the problems of growing up, an awareness of her developing body, and even the experience of first love.

At times she expresses the inner longings that color the adolescent's world so well that we almost forget the horror of the circumstances surrounding her:

"The sun is shining, the sky is deep blue, there is a lovely breeze and I'm longing — so longing — for everything. To talk, for freedom, for friends, to be alone ... I'm restless, I go from one room to the other, breathe through the crack of a closed window, feel my heart beating, as if it is saying, 'Can't you satisfy my longings at last?'"

From the "crack of her closed window" in her hiding place, Anne observed life and death and recorded both: "From my favorite spot I look up at the blue sky and the bare chestnut tree, on whose branches little raindrops shine, appearing like silver, and at the seagulls and other birds as they glide on the wind."

But she also saw "rows of good, innocent people accompanied by crying children, bullied and knocked about until they almost drop. No one is spared — old people, babies, expectant mothers, the sick — each and all join in the march of death."

The last entry in Anne's diary is dated August 1, 1944. Three days later, the Gestapo uncovered the Franks' hiding place and took the eight Jews at 263 Prinsengracht to Gestapo headquarters in Amsterdam. On September 3, the day the Allies captured Brussels, these eight were among the last shipment of a thousand Jews to leave Holland aboard a freight train, 75 people to a car. The cars were sealed. After three days and nights, the train reached Auschwitz in Poland, where the men and women were immediately separated. It was the last Otto Frank saw of his wife and daughters. Mrs. Frank was to die the following year, half-mad, at Auschwitz.

In October of 1944, Anne and her sister Margot were moved from Auschwitz to Belsen, a camp in Germany considered by many the most brutal of all. Miraculously, at Belsen, Anne found her best friend from Amsterdam, Lies Goosens. Lies, who survived Belsen, recalls the night when she and Anne met in the camp, separated by a barbed-wire fence: "I waited, shivering in the darkness. It took a long time. But suddenly I heard a voice: 'Lies, Lies? Where are you?'"

"It was Anne, and I ran in the direction of her voice, and then I saw her beyond the barbed wire. She was in rags. I saw her emaciated, sunken face in the darkness. Her eyes were very large. We cried and cried, for now there was only the barbed wire between us, nothing more. But I was in a block where we still occasionally had packages. Anne had nothing at all. She was freezing and starving."

Another survivor of Belsen recalls that Anne never lost her humanity; she still cried when they marched the gypsy children by on their way to the ovens. "She was," remembers Mrs. de Wiek, a former Belsen inmate, "one of the last to still cry. We scarcely saw and heard these things any longer. Something protected us, kept us from seeing. But Anne had no such protection, to the last. She cried. And you cannot imagine how soon most of us came to the end of our tears."

In February of 1945, Anne's sister Margot became gravely ill; she died at the end of the month or the beginning of March. Anne, who was also sick at the time, died in March of 1945. She was not yet 16.

The war in Europe ended just two months later and Belsen was liberated.

Anne Frank's voice speaks to us across the years with as much force and meaning as it did 45 years ago. It speaks to us of courage, compassion, strength and, above all, her ability to continue to love in the face of unspeakable inhumanity.

"I want to go on living even after my death," wrote Anne in her diary. There can be little doubt that her wish has been fulfilled. For the millions of people who have read a slim volume started by a 13-year-old girl in Amsterdam, the beautiful, glowing spirit of Anne Frank lives on. ⊕

ALICE STEINBACH

A Sense
Of Place

233

From the age of two, one of my most persistent companions has been homesickness. We met — homesickness and I — in the hospital during a lengthy stay, one during which I almost died. Separated as I was from my family, in pain and alone, a young child bewildered by what was happening, I became an early and ardent student of homesickness.

Growing up, I was drawn to books and stories that drew on dual themes: home and a sense of place as constants in one's life; or the fearful absence of any such deep and sustaining attachment. In my adolescence, I was near-obsessed with Charlotte Bronte's book, "Jane Eyre." Jane, an orphan, moved from the austere, punishing Lowood school to Thornfield Hall, the cold, gray home of the remote Mr. Rochester — a scenario I found more terrifying than Bram Stoker's "Dracula."

Out of fear, mostly, I became adept at making a home for myself from whatever material was at hand. Of course, there's nothing to compare to the home I now live in, a cozy, white-washed brick cottage surrounded by towering trees and century-old azaleas. But surely it's a sign of progress that recently I think more and more of the neighborhood in Paris — the 7th arrondissement, to be exact — that's becoming my home away from home.

Home

I was standing in the bathroom, admiring the new, flowered wallpaper, when suddenly the early morning sun hit at a wide, blinding angle through the window, lighting up the entire room.

Fascinated, I stood there surrounded by the sparkling white light, and I thought: How beautiful this room looks. It's like standing inside a diamond.

And then something odd happened. I began to walk from room to room in my house, looking at each one as if I'd never seen it before. And in the act of noticing old, familiar things in a new way, I experienced a deep sense of connection with this house that is my home.

Small things, usually taken for granted, began to rearrange themselves into new patterns of order and beauty: the oriental carpet floating across the polished shine of a dark, hardwood floor; the curved edge of a white marble table against a mimosa-colored wall; the arc of an outside tree branch framed like a photograph through the panes of a French window; the blue-and-white porcelain bowl filled with apples the color of pale emeralds.

I thought: How comfortable I feel here in this house. And how much of my emotional life, as well as my physical life, inhabits this space.

Even now, looking around, I find proof of this everywhere. There, in the dining room, I see a son on the night of his high school graduation. He is surrounded by friends and family and his face is flushed with excitement.

And, there in the kitchen, I see a son whistling as he whips up one of his specialties, "pot luck salad."

I spot my mother, too — sitting in an armchair, reading — a pale yellow afghan wrapped around her legs.

I see the cats — both past and present — everywhere. Sunning themselves on windowsills. Curled up on the kitchen floor in rectangles of light. Leaping onto a rocking chair.

Scenes of friends and family, gathered at the dining room table, assemble in my head. I hear the sound of wine corks popping. Loud guitar music drifts down from a son's bedroom. I smell a turkey cooking in the oven and see a family decorating a Christmas tree in the living room.

And as I watch and listen, what emerges from all these memories of those who live here, or have lived here, is one profound truth: This is our small place in the world, this house. And we are safe here because this house is also our home. It's a place where we can dream and cry and laugh and make mistakes. We belong here.

Whenever we "inhabit" a house, writes architect Witold Rybczynski, we make it come "alive" by filling it "not only with our activities and physical possessions, but also with our aspirations and dreams." And in this way, he continues, we "give identity to — and are identified with — our dwellings."

It is not a new idea to me — that a house inhabits us as much as we inhabit it. I have only to close my eyes and I am back in the house of my childhood.

It is raining outside and I am lying in my old bed with the maple headboard, staring up at the ceiling, at the little stars painted there by my father. There's a white Motorola radio next to the bed, and the "Let's

236

Pretend" theme music is playing. Downstairs, my mother is in the kitchen fixing breakfast. I smell bacon.

I used to call this kind of thought a "memory." But now I know it's more than a memory. It's me. That house, with all that transpired there, lives in me, just as I once lived in it.

It's a way of thinking that seems to run in the family.

For example, a letter arrived recently from a son in Japan. He writes: "Next week will mark one year since I left home. And while remembering such a date may seem trivial to some, it has a lot of meaning for me. Although I am happy with my life here, I would give almost anything sometimes just to sit in our backyard for five or ten minutes. Or to sleep in my room for one night. It's very easy to take the things we love for granted, isn't it?"

After reading this letter, I drifted into my son's bedroom. And sure enough, he was there, still inhabiting his old room.

Just as his old room, I suspect, now inhabits him in a small Japanese village halfway round the world.   ⊕

Familiar Strangers

People, I've noticed, often don't see things clearly until they've vanished. Oh, sure, we look at the world around us, but somehow we manage not to see it.

Until, as I said, whatever it is we've become accustomed to looking at suddenly disappears.

Take, for example, the woman I used to see — or look at — on my way to work each morning.

Here is how I remember her: a gray-haired, neatly attired woman, probably in her late 60s, always wearing a hat, and always waiting at the bus stop around 8 a.m.

I also remember that for three years, no matter what the weather, she was there at that corner. Appropriately dressed, of course.

In rainy weather, she wore a large rain hat and rubbers over her shoes.

On snowy days, heavy boots poked out from beneath her coat, and over her always-proper hat, she tied a woolen scarf.

Summertime brought out neat, belted cotton dresses, accessorized, naturally, by a straw hat that rode down low over her eyeglasses.

But regardless of what she wore, she gave off an air of competence coupled with a no-nonsense attitude. Clearly a working woman at an age when a lot of people no longer work, this was someone who telegraphed stability and dependability in a world that increasingly seems to contain less of both.

Of course, I remembered all this about the woman at the bus stop only after she vanished. It was then I realized how much I counted on seeing her each morning.

You might say I missed her.

Naturally, I had fantasies about her disappearance. Retirement? Accident? Or something worse? Now that she was gone, I felt I had actually known her.

And thinking about her in this way made me realize suddenly that a significant part of our daily life consists of such encounters with familiar strangers.

We all have them — these familiar strangers we see regularly:

The middle-aged power walker we see every afternoon at 3 p.m.

The woman who regularly walks her Yorkie at the crack of dawn.

The dapper twins — two brothers who appear to be in their 70s — we see at the library.

The slender, attractive man at the supermarket who, rain or shine, always wears sunglasses.

They are people we think we don't know — but actually do.

And such people are, I contend, important markers in the landscape of our lives: They add weight to our sense of place — weight to our sense of belonging in *that* place.

Think about it for a moment.

If, while driving to work, we mark where we are when passing a certain building or a certain intersection, why shouldn't we mark where we are when we pass a familiar, though unnamed, person on the street?

After all, if part of being a tourist is seeing nothing and no one familiar to you, then can we not say that seeing the familiar jogger or supermarket shopper is part of what makes us a citizen of our community?

It is one of the things an immigrant longs for, I suppose: the sight of the familiar stranger. The shopkeeper who nods to you. The bus driver who delivers you to your workplace each day. The woman you see from the bus each day walking her child to school.

Sometimes I wonder: Am I that person to someone? That familiar stranger?

Perhaps someone who shops at my supermarket every Saturday sees me there and — though not consciously — notes my presence. Or perhaps someone at the drugstore counter, where I often eat breakfast, would notice if I suddenly stopped showing up.

Once in a very great while, you might actually meet one of these familiar strangers. As I did a few months ago.

I was standing in a coffee shop when a woman walked up and said hello to me. "Do you know who I am?" she asked. And I did. She was a patient I had seen many times in my doctor's office. It was an easy, familiar exchange — although we never got around to exchanging names.

Here's what I remember most about the importance of familiar strangers. Once, driving home from the airport after a long vacation, I was feeling disoriented, out-of-place. Then I saw him: An elderly man dressed in a tweed jacket and green cap. I guess I'd seen this man walking through my neighborhood a thousand times.

"Ah," I thought, seeing this familiar stranger. "I'm home at last."

Fifth Grade

Suppose I write down the words: "Last week of school."

And suppose I remind you of how it threatened to go on forever, that last week before school closed for the summer vacation.

Of how you'd be sitting at your desk, sweating and sleepy, in a room turned white from the diamond-bright June sun blasting through the useless, tan window shades.

And of how every once in a while, just before you dozed off, a hot breeze would come through the open transom and swirl around the room, fluttering papers on desks and making the blinds go flap, flap, flap before it passed out through the window again.

And suppose I remind you that right now — even as you're remembering how the school custodian, Joe, always cut the grass during that last week, and of how Miss Parlett took to wearing white shoes — there are thousands of kids in thousands of classrooms who are daydreaming their way through the last week of school.

In fact, there is so much daydreaming going on among school-children this week that, if daydreams were hummingbirds, the air would be filled with whirring blurs of birds; they would hover above schools from coast to coast like a veil of summer desire.

Who does not remember that last week of school? Of what it's like to be a kid so dizzy with the idea of summer that you're oblivious to everything but the promise of freedom?

Like a sea-weary sailor trying to sight land, you sit slumped in your seat — the back of your clothes already sticking to the splintered wooden chair — and scan the horizon outside.

And when you tire of that, you watch, trance-like, as a trapped bumblebee bumps up against the window, trying to escape. In fact, it's a perfect metaphor; the last week of school always revolves around the theme of escape and freedom.

So intense is your concentration that you do not hear poor Miss Parlett, who is valiantly trying to review the main themes of "Ivanhoe." But you do notice that, in addition to the white shoes, Miss Parlett is wearing yellow enamel earrings shaped like small pansies.

It was the fifth grade, and that time in your life when summer was unconditionally … summer.

A time before summer jobs entered the picture.

A time before summer romances entered the picture.

A time before the conflicts of hanging out with your friends vs. hanging out with your family became a major summer drama.

A time when summer stretched out ahead of you like the Kansas prairies, endless and uncharted.

So you sat in Miss Parlett's class and dreamed of sleeping late and waking to the smell of sizzling bacon and newly mowed grass.

You dreamed of playing Monopoly and jacks on the screened-in porch which, because it was shaded by a huge elm tree, remained cool even on the hottest day.

You dreamed about wearing nothing but white shorts and halter tops. And you surprised yourself by realizing that summer is a time when feet come into their own: shoeless feet that know the pleasure of walking barefoot on damp sand, on cool grass, on rain-soaked asphalt.

You dreamed of fireworks and hot dogs — not the winter kind of hot dogs but the summer kind, grilled in the backyard and dripping with mustard and pickle relish.

You also dreamed of weekend trips in the family car: of starting out at 5 a.m. and stopping, ravenous, at 9 a.m. for breakfast at Howard Johnson's where, sitting on orange Leatherette seats in the booth, you'd eat pancakes and strawberries and maple syrup and, on the way out, stuff your pockets with pink and green mints from the candy dish next to the cash register.

But most of all, sitting in Miss Parlett's class during the last week of school, you'd dream of your first day at the pool: of the smell of baby oil and pale bodies and the sudden shyness that accompanied them.

You'd dream of that first contact with the water and the sensation of diving through a line that divided noise from silence, earth from water. Underwater, the sounds of volleyball players and the jukebox over at the lunch shack seemed eerily distant, as if they were coming from another planet.

You'd dream of how late in the afternoon, with the smell of chlorine heavy in your hair, you'd make the long, hot march back to the streetcar and the worn plastic seats that scratched your sunburn no matter how you arranged your body.

And then you'd dream of how, ever so gently, the steady rhythm of the wheels set you dozing.

Dozing just as you are now, in the fifth grade of Miss Parlett's class during the last week of school.   ⊕

My Neighborhood

Here in the neighborhood these days, life is good.

First of all, there's the simple beauty to be observed along the street: the last of the pearl-hued peonies still blooming, the grass lush from the rains, the striped green-and-white awning jutting out from a neighbor's porch like the prow of a ship, the late spring sun washing each house with a pale rose glow in the morning and a shadow of deep lavender in the late afternoon.

But beyond the temporal beauty to be found on my street, what makes life so congenial in the neighborhood is the sense of small-town values that thrive here; values that conjure up words like community, friends, neighborliness, roots, commitment.

Or put another way: values that embrace all the mysterious complexities that shape and inform the idea of Home.

A lot has been written about the place we call Home — although some would argue that Home is not a place but a state-of-mind. "Home," observed Robert Frost, "is the place where, when you go there, they have to take you in." But T.S. Eliot saw home not as a place to go back to, but as the very beginning of our self-identity: "Home is where one starts from," he wrote. "As we grow older/The world becomes stranger, the pattern more complicated."

And as the pattern grows more complicated, we find ourselves standing on a path farther and farther away from where we started out. We are presented with opportunities and choices in numbers undreamed of by past generations, and we move out and up, leaving behind our sense of roots.

In such a mobile culture — a mobility not only geographic but social and economic as well — not many people under the age of 50 or so can hope to emulate someone such as writer Eudora Welty, who since the 1920s has lived in the house built by her parents in Jackson, Miss. In an interview a few years ago, Welty spoke of how she loved to travel, but — and this is the important part — she also observed that her love of travel was fueled, in part, by the sweet, unshakable knowledge that eventually she would return Home.

The odd thing, it occurs to me, is that "homesickness" is experienced not only by those far away from home, but by those who have never had a home. Even homeless children, whose entire lives have been spent in shelters or some such, have expressed feelings of "homesickness." Once, in an interview at a homeless shelter, a nine-year-old girl told me her dream was to "live in a house with its own kitchen" and "to belong somewhere."

In the end, we all need to belong somewhere.

It's a phenomenon that may account, in part, for the success of the so-called "Ralph Laurenization" of America: Houses decorated to look like Old Money; the use of a Polo player (really, do you know anyone who plays polo?) to symbolize a style of life; $600 denim jackets made to look as old as America's long-gone Old West culture; stores designed to look like English manor houses.

But the longing for roots may be shifting. If you believe the cutting-edge, sociological wisdom, more and more people today are searching not so much for their past roots but for a place to put down *new* roots.

And so we come back to the beginning: Life in my neighborhood is good these days.

Although I do not live, as Eudora Welty does, in the house of my youth — many houses and rooms and hotels and apartments separate me from that — it nonetheless is the house where, for the last 10 years or so, I have put down my roots.

Home for me now is: the sight from my bedroom window of a neighbor's seven-year-old son studying a bird in its nest; it's Ben, the 6-foot, 1-inch (if he stands on his hind paws) Newfoundland puppy who greets me at my car; it's Peggy, the world's most timid cat, who occasionally ventures from her house to roam in my garage; it's the next-door father-and-son team that figured out how to get me back into my house when I'd locked myself out one night; it's the lush, full-blown roses brought to my back door by the retired couple across the alley.

And it's the grocery store across the street — and the drugstore and branch library — where everybody knows my name. Not to mention the pet shop where — if you're in need of a good laugh — you can always stop by to watch the poodles being bathed.

What more could you ask for in a neighborhood?

One more thing: Don't buy that "Good fences make good neighbors" philosophy. If you ask me, it's a lot simpler than that. Good neighbors make good neighbors. ⊕

Beyond Words

For the last 20 minutes, I've been trying to remember whether it was the philosopher Kierkegaard or my Aunt Claire who made this profound observation: "Everything is always about something else."

Regardless of who said it, the idea conveyed in that short, simple sentence is as relevant to our lives as any I can think of. Yet, perhaps because such a view implies chaos, it's an idea not often examined.

Now, however, there is a movie that portrays the sharp truth behind the assumption that "Everything is about something else." Based on Norman Maclean's autobiographical story, "A River Runs Through It" is a film that reminds us of how seldom we recognize what really binds a family together and shapes its memories. And of how important it is not to miss the meaning present in the moment of transaction between us and our children.

Indeed, moviegoers will leave this film understanding, in ways deeper than words, that verbal communication is often a poor vehicle for conveying one's truest and most essential nature.

On the surface, "A River Runs Through It" is a film about a

Presbyterian minister who is able to express his feelings only by teaching his sons the art of fly-fishing. Norman Maclean, who died in 1990, was one of the minister's sons. He suggests that one reason for writing a book about fly-fishing and his father was to let all children know what kind of people their parents are, or hope they are, or think they are.

Norman Maclean's son, John, listened to many of his father's stories before they were written. Writing them down, however, "was very, very hard" for his father, said John Maclean in a recent radio interview. "He spent 40 years telling a book that was about 104 pages long when he finished it."

Hearing this, it struck me that all of us, in the way we live our lives, are telling a book. Most of us will never write it down, but we will "tell" it to our children: in the way we spend time with them and in the way we allow them, or won't allow them, to share with us what we most value.

Words, of course, are capable of conjuring up childhood memories. I, for example, think of the thousands of stories my own grandmother told me during the first 10 years of my life: of her growing up in Scotland; of having her own pony; of living on the grounds of a castle; of losing a sister to scarlet fever.

I remember them all. But the memory of such spoken stories never really summons up my grandmother in quite the way that standing in my garden does.

Words have no dominion here among the snowdrops and lily-of-the-valley. Like a genie from a bottle, the smell of rich, damp earth releases my grandmother's essence, and she appears before me: a small, determined woman wearing sturdy shoes and gardening gloves.

Her father — my great-grandfather — had been head gardener to the Royal Family at a castle in Scotland. And it was clear from my grandmother's stories that the only closeness she ever shared with her strict father came when he allowed her to walk the gardens with him.

Gardening, I suppose you could say, became my grandmother's equivalent of fly-fishing. And at a very early age, I became her willing disciple.

Remembering my grandmother in the garden, I'm certain that Norman Maclean couldn't have loved the feel of a two-pound rainbow on the end of his line any more than my grandmother loved the feel of the earth opening up beneath her fingers.

But like Norman's father, she never conveyed in words her reverence for all this. As a child, I understood, without knowing I understood, that gardening was not something my grandmother did; it was what my grandmother *was*. When my grandmother knelt among the flowers, she was assuming her place in nature; she was affirming that there was order in the world, if one could only find the right river to stand in.

And over the many seasons of standing next to her in that river of rich earth and fragrant nature, I like to think some sense of her order, in what is essentially a chaotic world, passed into me.

And into one of my sons. In fact, I know it did, because I never pass by the yellow azalea or the blue hydrangea or the mountain laurel without thinking of the seasons he and I worked side by side in the garden.

249

Once, we ran out of daylight before we ran out of plants. So my son and I finished the job by flashlight. I remember talking very little in the fading light. But I also remember it as a night when more was said than I could ever say. ⊕

The Geography of Hope

Spring, 1985: The Year of Planting Dangerously.

Azaleas, lilies, peonies, lavender, iris, and a jewel-like, star-flowered Kousa dogwood; we planted them all, my 16-year-old son and I, that spring. How clearly I recall those April weekends when some intangible but urgent need gripped first my son, and then me, driving us back to the earth; to dig out the old, to plant the new, and then to watch and wait in silent companionship as our garden unfolded slyly after nights of spring rains and days of high, warm sunlight.

It was odd, the way some sharp force of nature briefly pierced both our lives that spring, demanding, it seemed, that my son and I renew our connections to the natural world.

Of course, man's primitive need to commune with nature — and his awe in the face of such deep instincts — is long established and well documented. Here, for example, is Thoreau writing in 1848 from the Maine Woods:

"Talk of mysteries! Think of our life in nature — daily to be shown matter, to come in contact with it — rocks, trees, wind on our cheeks! The solid earth! The

actual world! Contact! Contact! Who are we? Where are we?"

And here is Gretel Ehrlich writing in "The Solace of Open Spaces" (1985) of how she recovered from a lover's death by seeking out the comforting emptiness of the Wyoming plains. "Everything in nature invites us constantly to be what we are," wrote Ehrlich, a filmmaker who left behind her urban environment to find in nature the self she had lost through a loved one's death.

A sojourn in the Maine woods; a retreat to the Wyoming plains; the planting of a small garden by a 16-year-old boy and his mother. Acts that suggest, perhaps, an attempt to connect with something larger; to place oneself in the web of life that holds together the natural world.

But every year we are reminded that the web grows ever more fragile. Concerned environmentalists point to the high price we are paying for technological advances which, in the name of progress, have altered our relationship to nature.

Simply put, the thesis is: As man progresses, nature declines.

In a book mournfully titled "The End of Nature," Bill McKibben goes even further, arguing that we "have deprived nature of its independence, and that is fatal to its meaning. Nature's independence is its meaning; without it there is nothing but us."

By altering the earth into something man-made and artificial, he believes, we are risking not only environmental disaster but the loss of our spiritual connection to nature:

"[When] the temperature and rainfall are no longer to be entirely the work of some separate, uncivilizable force, but instead in part a product of our habits, our economies, our ways of life. ... the world outdoors will mean the same thing as the world indoors, the hill the same thing as the house."

Spring, 1985: The night before my mother died, there was a fierce ice storm. It shrouded the cars on the hospital parking lot with a thin, white glaze. The overhead telephone wires shone in the moonlight like carnival lights strung across a high, silvery sky; the trees groaned (or was it a sigh?) under the weight of their glistening, iced branches.

It was so beautiful, so completely a thing of nature's making —

unaccountable to man or time or the cycles of life and death — that I
ran back into the hospital to tell my mother about it. Her room over-
looked a large evergreen magnolia tree, and through the window we
watched in silence as the ice storm enfolded the tree within its sheets of
whiteness.

To tell you the truth, I was remembering that night when my son
and I planted the Kousa dogwood later that spring. Standing beneath its
silvery branches and looking up into the profusion of star-shaped, white
flowers, I thought of snow, of ice, of my mother looking at the tree, her
last tree, just outside her window.

Now it is outside my window.

I believe it was Wallace Stegner who described nature as "part of the
geography of hope." Perhaps it was the need to restore that hope that
accounted for the planting frenzy my son and I experienced that spring.

But who can explain such gossamer connections? Not all the Earth
Day pamphlets or environmental books in the universe can answer such
mysteries as Thoreau's cry of: *Who are we? Where are we?*

But this we know: Part of the answer lies in the unfolding of the
rose; in the silence of the snow; in the flash of a firefly in the night; in the
web of life that binds man and nature together on a small planet called
Earth. ⊕

ALICE STEINBACH

As Time Goes By

A postcard arrives with the following message:

Dear Mom,

It's three in the morning and I'm on a train going from Berlin to Paris. It's dark on the train right now — everyone is trying to sleep — and I am writing this under a small, overhead light. I've met so many interesting people on the trains here in Europe and seen the most spectacular sights. Will write soon. Take care.

I see him now, the sender of this card: a long, lanky American boy hunched under a small writing light, scratching out shaky words on a postcard as a train hurtles through the night. In my mind, it takes on the shape of an Edward Hopper painting: Standing outside of the train, I look through the window at the solitary figure illuminated by a single shaft of light.

He's on his way to Japan, this son, to temporarily take up life there. The other son is in Colorado, in graduate school, living in a house with two other students. From him, I get postcards from Aspen and Telluride and the Canadian Rockies. Of course, it used to be the other way around: I was the one mailing letters and postcards to my sons — from such faraway places as Paris and Mexico. When, I wondered, had it all changed?

Without my noticing it, the clock has moved me farther away from something, and closer toward something else. Still, I can hear that clock ticking as loudly as ever; a good sign, I think, that time is still on my side.

September Song

It's amazing how quickly it all happens: the days suddenly turning shorter, the leaves going red on the dogwood tree, the sunlight slanting in through the windows at a different angle, the need for a thin blanket at night.

Then one day you notice that the garden seems quite still, no longer alive and growing. And you're aware that your summer clothes feel all wrong — the colors too light, the shoes too bare. Porches start to look emptier and the air doesn't seem as fragrant with the smell of steaks sizzling on grills.

And if you listen carefully, you can almost hear the faint sound of a door closing. As it swings shut, we catch our last glimpses of the flowers and the warmth and the brilliant light of that high, bold season we call summer.

Why does the end of summer always catch us by surprise? Why is it that we're never prepared for the abruptness with which the shortened day bumps up against the lengthened evening? Or for the psychological shift that comes as one season ends and another begins?

True, summer isn't officially over until late September, but for most of us the fall season begins just after the Labor Day weekend.

It begins with the kids going back to school. With the packing of lunches and driving of car pools. With brand-new pencil cases and little pink erasers that give off the smell of new rubber.

It begins with saying "Hurry up or we'll be late" at least a dozen times a day.

It begins with heading the car out of the alley, only to find the street jammed with cars — the same street, incidentally, that only a week ago was almost deserted.

It begins with packing away the bathing suits that smell of chlorine and getting out the sweaters and jackets.

It begins with loading up the car with stereos and clothes and bean-bag chairs and driving your teen-ager off to a new life in some distant dormitory.

It begins with coming back to your teen-ager's empty room and, with a lump in your throat, wondering where the years went.

It begins with looking out your kitchen window and noticing how the leaves are scattered into zigzagged patterns across the lawn.

It begins with noticing how early the dark comes on and how, after dinner, the streets are no longer filled with the sounds of children playing.

It begins with the crunching sound of a small patch of leaves underfoot and the faint aroma of burning wood in the air.

If you're anything like me, fall begins with the melancholy feeling that something has been lost.

It's odd. I've had this feeling of loss about summer's end since I was a child but never knew why. But I can actually pinpoint its origins almost to the day and hour:

I was eight-years-old, sick with a strep throat and in my third day of missing the first week of school. The white Motorola radio next to my bed was on and suddenly a man's voice started singing: "And the days dwindle down to a precious few — September, November ..."

I didn't know who was singing or what the song was — years later I learned it was Frank Sinatra and "September Song" — but I knew instantly it was about loss and that it made me feel terribly sad.

It still does.

As you grow older, I suppose it's natural to notice the changing of the seasons and, perhaps, feel that inexplicable sadness. Maybe it's the dim recognition that there's a finite number of summers and falls left in your life.

A friend who's approaching her 85th year tells me that some years ago she began numbering the seasons. It helps her to understand, she says, how unique each one is. By her arithmetic, this year marks her 85th observance of the changing of summer into fall.

I thought about that the other evening as I stood outside watering my garden. "Look," an inner voice seemed to be saying, "look around you and take it all in. The setting sun forming pale rectangles on the brick wall. The clouds, veiled puffs of lavender, moving across the darkening sky like celestial sailboats. The gentle movement in the trees as unseen squirrels fly from branch to branch. The golden hue surrounding the last of the tall, black-eyed Susans."

Standing there, in the half-light of evening with summer all around me, I wanted to reach out, extend my arms, catch the warmth and the breeze and the flowers, and draw it all into a circle inside myself, where it could live forever.   ⊕

Stars

O ccasionally in everyone's life, a thought will surface, and that thought will act as a key: one that unlocks the past and pushes you through a door back to the half-forgotten memories of your childhood.

Sometimes, if the connections are strong enough — and your defenses weak enough — the view through the door is totally unobstructed. What you see is the clear, unbroken line that runs from here to there, from present to past; a line connecting the adult you are with the child you were. Then for a few minutes, you are gifted with the ability to see, feel, and think as you saw, felt, and thought in those early formative years.

For me, some events are guaranteed to trigger thoughts that act as express-lane connectors to my past: a visit to an amusement park I frequented as a child, slow-dancing in a dimly lit room to the music of Nat "King" Cole, the sight of my old elementary school playground, the fragrance of White Shoulders, a perfume I used throughout my high school years.

But sometimes the mind insists on going through a series of seemingly random associations to get you to whatever it is you're trying to locate in the past — a process which is sort of analogous to those connect-a-dot pictures, where you have to draw a line between the dots to find the figure hidden within.

This happened to me last week on a day when I was at home in bed, sick with the flu. Between dozing on and off, I read an account of how astronomers at the Space Telescope Institute in Baltimore recently produced the largest star atlas ever made.

Sixty times more detailed than any night-sky atlas (the previous one mapped a skimpy 250,000 celestial objects), the new "Guide Star Catalog" took eight years to amass and shows nearly 19 million stars. The atlas, written on computer discs, is so large that, if printed, would fill 400 volumes and weigh one ton.

The article pointed out that the map is a crucial component for the Hubble Space Telescope. By using nearby stars as landmarks — or more appropriately, skymarks — astronomers are able to point the telescope with greater accuracy and keep it locked on objects being studied.

259

Reading this, I suddenly remembered a story told to me several years ago by a 90-year-old gentleman from Southern Maryland. In eloquent, vivid language, he described to me his memories of seeing Halley's comet. The year was 1910 and he described, as if it were yesterday, how as a young man he stood on the banks of a river and saw *two* Halley's comets; one in the darkened, ash-black sky above and one reflected in the silver-gray river flowing past him.

As he described it, a clear image formed in my mind. It is an image that remains there today.

Now another image enters: That of my son at age 14. We are standing late at night in a field under a skyful of stars. My son, the amateur astronomer, has set up his telescope and is giving me a guided tour of the heavens. It's winter and it's cold; when he turns to tell me how to locate Arcturus, his breath makes frosty circles in the air. Even in the dark, I see his eyes are as bright as the North Star. They are my father's eyes.

My father loved the stars, too. Stars, he used to tell me, are best seen from the deck of a ship at sea.

Once, when I was little — and just home from a frightening stay in the hospital — my father painted the ceiling of my room with stars that glowed when the lights were turned off. It was an attempt to help me overcome my fear of the dark.

And it worked.

I can still remember how I would lie in bed at night and look up at the ceiling toward all those friendly, glowing stars. In fact, if I close my eyes right now, I can see that over to the right of the window is the fig-ure of Leo the Lion; near the closet door is the Big Dipper; and directly above my bed is the Big Dog, a constellation which, my father told me over and over, contains Sirius, the friendly Dog Star.

He always emphasized the word *friendly*.

Funny, isn't it, how one thought leads to another? A grown woman recovering from the flu, dozing on and off, can read about 19 million stars being stored on 400 computer discs and, as a result, find herself thinking this:

Although there were probably no more than 50 stars painted on that bedroom ceiling, to a little girl lying in the dark, it seemed like 19 million. ⊕

Spending Time

The man sitting next to me at the busy lunch counter was visibly annoyed. "I've been waiting over five minutes," he said, turning to me. "How long does it take to put some soup in a bowl and carry it out here?"

Too long, apparently.

The man who mistook his waitress for a servant got up and left in a huff. But not before unloading a parting shot: "Time is money," he said in an angry voice, one loud enough to be heard by everyone at the counter.

It was the second time I'd heard the same philosophy expressed that week: Time is money.

The first time I heard it was when a very impatient woman ended a phone conversation this way: "Well, I've got to go now. Time is money, you know."

The woman on the phone, by the way, was me.

Funny, isn't it, how sometimes you don't realize the stupidity of what you're saying until you hear someone else saying it?

Which is exactly what happened to me.

"What a stupid thing to say," I found myself thinking after the man at the lunch counter unleashed his "Time is money" bromide. Still, I knew I'd uttered those very words more times than I cared to admit. And so have many of my friends.

The fact is we live in a world inhabited by busy people. And busy people are usually kept busy by, among other things, the need to make money.

Which means a lot of our time gets equated with money. In that sense, I suppose, time *is* money.

But while most of us have a pretty clear idea of how hard it is to make money and how easy it is to spend it, we seem unable to extend this understanding to the concept of time.

Oh, we pay lip service to the idea of time as something to be spent — as in, "One of these days, I'm going to get around to spending more time with the kids." But we don't think of time as we do of money, as something that comes in limited quantities.

"Plenty of time to do that next year," we tell ourselves about the plan to replant the garden or to take an evening art class.

Time, you might say, has been on my mind lately.

I even looked it up in the dictionary:

"An indefinite, unlimited duration in which things are considered as happening in the past, present, or future," is the way *Webster's New World Dictionary* defines time.

For some reason, my next instinct was to look up the word "timeless." It was defined by *Webster's* as "that which cannot be measured by time."

Too much of life, I decided, is "measured by time." Or, to be precise, too much of *my* life.

And the joke's on me. Because I remember very little of the "measured time" — the minutes, hours, weeks, months, years — I spent trying to beat the clock.

But the timeless experiences exist still. And they are as clear and sharp in my memory as they were in actuality.

Here, for example, comes the memory of a night spent last summer in Oxford, England learning how to dance the quick step. For who-knows-how-long, a group of us — under the spell of Bruce, the dance instructor — glided, dipped, swooped and laughed our way across the wooden floors of Lincoln College. Time simply disappeared.

Afterward, walking home in the soft night air to my room at the college — the domes and spires of Oxford stabbing the dark blue sky above — I felt completely relaxed. I glanced at my watch and suddenly realized that for the last several hours I had not been measuring time.

And yet, I am able to relive the single moments of that singular evening as if they were happening right now.

It's the same with the memories of the spring when my 16-year-old son and I planted a garden together.

For my entire two-week vacation, I woke up with just one thought in my head: Lilacs. Or day lillies. Or snapdragons.

That was the spring my son and I told time by the position of the sun and our calculations as to how long we could dig and plant before darkness fell.

There are April mornings still when I wake up and think: I can smell the lilacs off in the distance of May.

So here is what I have decided time is:

Time, in the final analysis, is all we really have.

And the wise person will spend wisely the time of her life.   ⊕

Scents and Sensibility

E very once in a while, I'll stand next to someone who's wearing Shalimar perfume, and the scent of it will stop me dead in my tracks — really, dead in my tracks.

I will stand there, impaled on the past like a trophy butterfly, quite unable to think of anything except my mother, who wore only Shalimar perfume. It's the smell that, as a child, woke me up in the morning and put me to bed at night. It has the power to evoke my mother's essence more sharply than any photograph ever could.

Friends report similar experiences: moments when a scent or odor suddenly hurled them back across the years to some instantly familiar place.

A man I know speaks passionately of his feelings whenever he smells a well-worn, leather catcher's mitt. "God, it's like I'm 10 years old again and back in the old neighborhood, playing on the lot near Allendale Street," he says.

And this from a woman: "I have some of my mother's pressed powder, which smells like the dresser drawer she kept it in. Opening the compact instantly reminds me of her."

For another, it's the smell of tar that uncorks the genie of memory: "When I visited my grandmother one summer, they were tarring her street, and since then I've never smelled tar without thinking instantly of my grandmother," this woman says now.

Of all the senses, scientists say that smell is the most elemental. It is capable of immediately triggering powerful emotions undiluted by language or intellect.

This is so, writes Diane Ackerman in her book, "A Natural History of the Senses," because the nose is the only sense organ that "sends a message straight into the limbic system, a mysterious, ancient and intensely emotional section of our brain in which we feel, lust and invent."

While we all share this sensory ability, a recent study suggests that, generationally, we do not share the same set of nostalgia-triggering odors.

In other words, the generation gap that exists in such areas as music (think Frank Sinatra vs. Hammer) and technology (think records vs. compact discs) also exists when it comes to memory-evoking scents. At least that is what Alan R. Hirsch of the Smell and Taste Treatment Research Foundation concludes from a survey he conducted.

Here's a sampling of some of the generational differences he turned up. See if you can detect the major fault line that divides the generations.

For people born in the 1920s, '30s and '40s, some of the most nostalgia-evoking scents were: hot chocolate, Cracker Jack, lilies, cut grass, cinnamon, ocean air, hay, honeysuckle, manure, attics, baking bread, soap, clover, tweed, meatballs, split pea soup, fresh air, burning leaves, violets, and roses.

For those born in the '60s and '70s, the list went like this: Play-Doh, chlorine, marijuana, tuna casserole, Downy fabric softener, smoke, airplane fuel, disinfectant, motor oil, tacos, Cocoa Puffs, Windex, hair spray, refineries, SweeTARTS, plastic, suntan oil, scented Magic Markers, mosquito repellent, candy cigarettes, and burning tires.

Give yourself a score of 100 if you observed that, in the older generation, most of the memory-evoking scents fell into the "natural" category as opposed to the more "artificial" scents selected by the younger generation.

Still, there's no doubt in my mind that, in terms of nostalgia, one person's memory of the smell of airplane fuel equals another person's memory of the scent of baking bread.

A Baptist minister, whose name I can't remember, once observed that after a man makes a visit to his boyhood town, he finds that it wasn't the old home he wanted, but his boyhood.

Something similar happens, I think, when we tap into our deep, primitive limbic system through the sense of smell.

We realize, for instance, that when we are stopped dead in our tracks by a whiff of salt air and sea, it's not the weekend at the beach we want back, but everything that went with it: the station wagon loaded up with coolers and beach chairs, Dad driving and Mom in the front seat pouring lemonade from a Thermos into paper cups, the musty smell of the beach house, the sand on our bare feet, the spray of a wave at our back.

To put it another way, when we smell the sea air and salt water as adults, what we want back is ourselves — ourselves as we used to be.

But a little of this goes a long way. You can't go around getting stopped dead in your tracks too often.

Which is why I have never been able to wear Shalimar perfume.

Signs of Life

N ow that it's over, the thing I remember most about January is this: It went by in a blur.

In January, there were so many things, great and small, competing for our attention. The terrible events in Somalia, Bosnia, and Iraq. The crime rate here at home. The ever-ballooning deficit. The deaths of Thurgood Marshall and of Audrey Hepburn, Dizzy Gillespie, Rudolph Nureyev. Keeping up with the Clinton Cabinet. The Zoe problem. The Hillary factor. Inaugural balls. Christmas bills.

And, of course, the unthinkable: the demise of the Sears catalog.

January, in other words, was a lot like your typical pile-up in a rear-end collision: Just one event crashing into another. Without any warning.

Now the month is over. And I suddenly realize something important: That I blew it. I blew the entire month of January!

Looking back, I see that 31 days of my life have come and gone, and, try as I might, I don't really remember any of them. Not, at least, in any meaningful way.

Instead, when I think of January, all that comes to mind is work and grocery shopping and getting estimates on the leaking roof and trying to find out if there were termites in my garage.

The truth is, I got so caught up in the hectic pace of my day-to-day life — or "lifestyle" as it's now called — that I can't remember if it snowed in January, nor whether my closest friend just left on a trip or returned from one.

Worst of all, so immersed was I in my lifestyle this past month that I only remembered a son's birthday in the nick of time.

You'd think that almost forgetting a son's birthday would send a message, wouldn't you? The message being, one assumes, to look a bit more carefully at the life — I mean, lifestyle — you're living.

But oddly enough, it wasn't the close call with the son's birthday that forced me to look at January and realize that I had blown it.

It was seeing the daffodils.

It was coming home from work on a Friday, bone-tired, and seeing in the afternoon's fading light the bright green shoots in my garden. Without thinking, I dropped my briefcase and got down on my knees to examine the shoots. There were clumps of dirt riding their tops — visible reminders of the force with which the shoots had erupted through the hard earth of winter.

Signs of life, I thought, studying the slightly thickened tips that hinted of yellow. Not signs of lifestyle, but genuine signs of life. Suddenly, I felt lighter. The air seemed more buoyant to me, more supportive, somehow.

Then one thing led to another — as things always do if we allow the time for it — and pretty soon I was noticing my cat Max.

Old and thin now, Max was obviously enjoying the late-day sun of a surprisingly mild January day. I studied him.

Lying on the grass, his long, tiger-striped tail curved around his body, he looked almost young again. The beautiful symmetry of his curved body and tail disguised his boniness, disguised the fact that in Max the signs of life were waning.

But not on this day. On this day, he was stirred to action by the sight of a squirrel. His mouth twitched and strange sounds growled deep in his throat as he watched the squirrel jump from tree branch to tree branch. His green eyes glittered in the sun.

I guess I'd seen Max do this a thousand times: line up his target in those emerald eyes of his. But never before had I felt the urgent need to commit to memory these signs of life in Max.

Watching, I saw a blue jay fly by, a slash of deep blue against the thin blueness of the sky. Max was not distracted.

From the corner of my eye I saw my briefcase, upended in the winter grass where I had dropped it. Signs of lifestyle, I thought. It looked strange — my briefcase holding all its important papers. It looked as if a tiny alien spaceship had landed in my garden.

The cat is on his way out, I thought; the daffodils on their way in.

All of us are coming and going — saying hello and goodbye.

The world is turning even as I stand here, I thought. And we are all coming from or heading toward infinity. The cat, the squirrel, the bluejay, the daffodil. And me.

But unlike me they know nothing of infinity or ambition or lifestyle. They know only that they are drawn to the sun, to the hunt, to the tree, to the sky.

Drawn, in other words, to all the signs that point to life itself.   ⊕

269

The Middle Ages

Generally speaking, I don't eavesdrop on other people's conversations. But sometimes a sentence drifting into earshot is so provocative it compels me to drop whatever I'm thinking and to listen.

Take, for instance, the following dialogue between two women changing their clothes after a workout at a health club:

"I hate getting older, don't you?"

"Yeah. I'd give anything to be young again."

"Me too. I can't believe I'm thirty. Middle age really is the pits."

Well, I suppose you could make a case that everything in life, as Einstein was fond of pointing out, is relative — up to and including one's idea of when youth ends and middle age begins. I should add, however, that once past the age of 40, the line of demarcation between the two becomes much clearer: Middle age begins at whatever age you're going to be five years from now.

Few people, it seems, look forward to middle age and its dreaded companion, the much ballyhooed "mid-life crisis." Friends often tell me they see middle age as a point in the arc of life where you stop ascending and start declining.

To which I say: Lighten up! Which, actually, is a pretty good summation of what middle age can be. Lighter, somehow; less burdened by the confusion of adolescence and the desire and ambition of young adulthood. In fact, I would compare the feelings of middle age to those of being young if being young were more fun than it actually is.

Youth is a tricky thing; it's the rare person who can carry it off. Young people care too much about too many things; every tiny misstep is perceived as the end of the world, the descent into the pit from which there is no return. Youth is about intensity.

Middle age, on the other hand, can be a breeze; a time when life organizes itself into surprising patterns of lightness and grace and gentle revelations. A friend describes it as "a time when you locate parts of your nature that were submerged in youth." Middle age is about acceptance.

So what gives me the right to pontificate?

I know all this and feel free to pass it along because middle age brings with it the freedom to be wrong — sometimes completely wrong — without going into a tailspin about what people think. Maybe you don't agree with me. So sue me. The point is: Although I'd rather be perceived as correct in my approach to life, I can live with the knowledge that not everyone will agree with me. In the end, it is me, not you, who has to inhabit my life. I didn't know that when I was young.

271

This brings me to my new credo; the words that guide me when faced with the daily decisions that ultimately define a life. "If not now, then when?"

In other words, a person gets to a certain age and time starts to look more finite. If you don't do it now, when *are* you going to do it?

In my own life, such a philosophy accounts for a recent return to piano lessons; a new, part-time teaching job; a bedroom painted in pale golden yellows; a willingness to reveal more of myself to friends; and a real energy expended, to quote Thoreau, towards "affecting the quality of each day, which is the highest of arts."

Small steps, perhaps, but deeply satisfying ones. To me, that is. You, of course, will have to locate what satisfies you.

The trick to a satisfying life, someone once said, is what one empha-sizes. We either make ourselves miserable or we make ourselves strong. The amount of work is the same.

Along those lines, here are some things I no longer emphasize: I'm not as angry. I no longer pay homage to the concept known as quality time; all time is now quality time to me. I'm less critical of others and of myself. I'm less frightened of making a mistake.

What I like about being middle-aged (there, I said it!) is that I'm younger now than when I was young. I'm also older — a nice trait which allows me to experience the very real pleasure of enjoying younger people. I'm zanier. I'm taking more risks and holding less back. I love my friends for who they are and not who I'd like them to be.

And here's a big one: I've learned the value of laughter, of playful-ness, of the lightness of being.

Finally, of the two or three things I know about life, the most remarkable, perhaps, is that time really does fly when you're having fun. ⊕

Before Air Conditioning

T here was a time in summers past when people flocked to a movie not because it starred Arnold Schwarzenegger or Robocop but because of three little words posted on the marquee:

IT'S COOL INSIDE.

Usually it was a last-minute act of desperation that drove whole families out of their sticky, non-air-conditioned houses in search of a cool place to sit — or sleep — for a couple of hours. The entertainment merits of the movie or its actors were never an issue; the critical factor was the temperature inside the theater.

Because of reasoning such as this — and a stretch of August weather when whole days seemed like high noon — I had the good fortune as a child of being the first in my crowd to see the scintillating "Mission to Moscow." Three times. Once with my mother. Once with my grandmother. Once with my mother, grandmother and brother.

To escape the suffocating afternoon heat, we'd go to the 2 o'clock show and stay to see the 60-minute movie twice. (This was before movies metamorphosed into 2 1/2-hour "films.") What with the news-

reel and cartoon and, if you were lucky, a travel film about the economy
in the Azore Islands, it would be hovering around dinner time when you
left to hit the steamy streets.

Then after walking home — very slowly — and taking the fourth
shower of the day, we'd sit down to a cold supper of chicken and maca-
roni salad set out on the side porch. After supper, we'd get out the hose
and run barefoot through the wet grass, inventing water games that usually involved some sort of attack-and-escape theme. Often, our dazed-
looking dog and resentful cats would join in, vying for the cool spray of
water that made such a graceful arc as it jetted out of the hose.

Sleeping was always touch-and-go in such weather. On muggy
nights, when the air was still and the bedroom seemed suffocatingly hot,
there was always the pull-out sofa in the club basement. The other choice
was the glider on the porch. Not bad, if you could stand the mosquitoes.

Yes, we did things differently back in the old days, the days before air
conditioning changed the way we live. Which, when you stop and think
about it, wasn't that long ago.

I'm always surprised when it's pointed out that home air conditioning didn't really take off until the late 1950s. From sales of 74,000 home
units in 1948, the home unit market grew to only about 6 million in
1962. Now, two-thirds of all new homes built in the United States come
equipped with air conditioning.

In a fascinating book published a few years ago, the editors of
Consumer Reports cast their votes for the 50 most important consumer
items of the last 50 years — the ones that fundamentally changed the
way we live.

Called "I'll Buy That," the book singles out such life-altering
advances as television, frozen food, automatic washers and dryers, personal
computers, jet travel, and our old friend, air conditioning.

In fact, air conditioning is the first product mentioned in the book.
Contending that air conditioning changed our lives as dramatically as any
modern-day invention, the authors write: "Without air-conditioning, we
wouldn't have jet air travel, manned space flight, submarines or comput-

ers ... or Miami, Houston, or Los Angeles."

Still, there are those who say we've lost something with the advent of air conditioning. They say that, because of it, there's no sense of place now — that you can't tell the difference between summer in Houston and summer in Seattle.

And they say that air conditioning has separated us from the heart-beat of nature. Instead of hearing the cicadas at high noon and the crickets in the evening grass, the sound of summer is now the droning white noise of the omnipresent air conditioner.

And there are some who mourn the loss of seersucker suits and folks sitting on the front steps at twilight while their children play games on the lawn or in the street.

Remember? You could hear the sound of voices talking to one another up and down the block and then, in the darkening light, there'd be the flare of a match struck against the sidewalk, followed by the fragrance of pipe smoke that drifted down the street like a scented cloud.

And, later, lying in your bed with all the windows open, you'd listen to the sweet hum of familiar voices coming from the porch below until finally the voices stopped and the last sound you heard before drifting off to sleep was the screen door slapping shut.

Remember? ⊕

Better-Late-Than-Never Mail

S o, I thought, standing at my mailbox, how many bills did I get today? How much junk mail? How many "free" gift offers of land in Florida or burial plots in Western Maryland?

Nowadays, more often than not, it's extremely irksome to go through one's mail: Letter-writing has all but vanished from the culture (today Elizabeth Barrett Browning would fax her letters to Robert and he would answer her via his cellular car phone), and so have thank-you notes and most other civilized forms of personal mail.

Today would be no different, I figured, as I riffled through the glossy Christmas catalogs, supermarket offerings, and missives addressed either to "Occupant" or someone named Mrs. Frances Sweeney. (I've gotten occasional pieces of Mrs. Sweeney's mail for the last 10 years; I can only assume she occupied my house prior to my moving in.)

But then I saw it: Tucked between the House of Foam catalog and the 50-cents-off-a-large-pizza coupon was this plain, manila-colored postcard — the kind you buy from the post office for strictly utilitarian purposes. The small, cramped handwriting on the back looked vaguely familiar to me. No. Suddenly it looked *very* familiar to me.

It was, in fact, my son's handwriting.

I quickly turned the postcard over and saw that my son had sent it from Cabin 12 of Camp Minnehaha, located in Minnehaha Springs, W.Va. Receiving this postcard was quite a shock to me — this particular son is currently attending college in New England. In fact, I had talked to him just that morning and he somehow had made no mention of having transferred from Williams College to Camp Minnehaha.

My eyes moved to the postcard. It was dated June 28, 1980.

1980! Huh? I thought.

I sucked in my breath. Was I caught in some kind of strange time warp? Or was I traveling, no, hurtling back into a time zone where I was younger, my kids were younger, and life was slow and oh so mellow?

Naaaaahhhh.

It was just the post office again, doing what it does. Whatever that is.

But I did feel a little bit like Nancy Drew as I studied the mysterious postcard. I analyzed it the way Nancy might have analyzed the Clue in the Crumbling Wall. Or the Mystery of the Brass-Bound Trunk. The postcard, I noted, was in pristine condition. No signs of having been folded, mutilated or kicked around in bad weather. The semi-hard manila paper showed not the slightest sign of wear.

Next, I observed, there were no additional postmarks on the card. Just June 28, 1980. Oh, and a second look revealed that it had been mailed in the morning.

Perhaps I would find a clue in the message penned on the back. (As I recall, that's how Nancy Drew cracked the Secret at Larkspur Lane.) Here's some of what was written on the postcard. Only the name of my son has been changed and some parts deleted, to protect the innocent:

Dear Mom,

People in my cabin are very nice and everyone has a nickname. One nickname for a kid named Brian is Bubbles. I thought I had lost my baseball glove but I found it after being VERY scared. I don't need soap anymore, but if you've already sent it, I could always use more. I do need that mess kit though.

David and I are going to play golf after rest period. My cabin is in an uproar right now because my counselor isn't here. I got two of your letters. Do the cats miss me? Today is Friday and camp is almost 1/2 over. I've gotten to sleep real well except for one night. Have you gotten my other two letters?

Love, Sam

I felt a lot of things while reading this nine-year-old postcard from an 11-year-old boy who figures quite prominently in my life. And one was the dissolving of time. Someone once pointed out, or maybe I made it up myself, that memory is nothing more than the daring rearrangement of time in the imagination. Nothing more than a reordering of experience and observation.

And so it was that time rearranged itself daringly as I read the tiny, familiar handwriting: I saw with vivid clarity the 11-year-old boy boarding the bus with his friend, David, setting out for the unknown; for this place far away in West Virginia called Camp Minnehaha. They both hated the name.

I felt both happy and sad reading the postcard, that bittersweet combination of feelings that becomes a more frequent visitor as you grow older. But above all, I felt deeply grateful to the United States Postal Service for giving me back — temporarily, at least — my son at the wonderful, sweet, tender, funny, unforgettable age of 11.   ⊕

ALICE STEINBACH

Departures

Looked at in a certain way, one of life's truest realities is this: We are all coming and going, saying hello and goodbye, letting go of people and things that we are not ready to let go of.

But in memory, we can rescue the people and things we loved from the vast blankness of loss. I remember, for instance, a long-ago New Year's Eve:

I am eight-years-old and the sounds of the party downstairs have awakened me. I hear my mother's laugh and my father's voice floating above the noise. Still half-asleep, I creep down the stairs and out onto the back porch. It had snowed earlier and the moonlight pours down on the glazed crust of ice covering the grass. I watch as our gray-and-white cat, Mittens, walks delicately on top of the ice, his tail plumed up towards the stars, his paws breaking through the thin ice with a crisp, crunching sound. Inside my house, I hear the people counting down: Five, four, three, two, one. Happy New Year! And suddenly my father is at my side; he picks me up, lifting me high into the air. My father's face, backlit by the moon, swims in memory; smiling, strong.

They're gone now, most of those who were there the night a young girl stood beneath a starry sky listening to the crunch of a cat's paw and the ice creaking in the birch tree. But as each comes forth in memory, I remember the light that shone out of them. Nancy, Shelby, Maggie, Mittens — Mother, Father, Grandmother and the cat who walked on ice — all of them are gone now. But in my life, I loved them all.

The Girl Who Loved Cats & Flowers

E arly in the autumn of 1984, my mother — for no apparent reason
— began writing down the story of her life. A fit and energetic woman
in the seventh decade of her life, she laughingly referred to these writings
as "my book," and her desire to put down her thoughts and memories
became something of a minor obsession.

Once, when she turned down a dinner invitation, telling me she had
to work on her book, I seem to remember laughing at her diligence and
asking her where the fire was.

The fire, as it turned out, was inside her. She finished her book in
early December. Three months later, she was dead.

From my mother's book:

*My deepest values are being honest and behaving in a gentle way. I have
loved my family, friends, nature (how beautiful the world is!), animals, music and
so many other things. It will be hard to say goodbye to the people I love and the
beauty (violets, anemones, lilac, lily of the valley, freesia, roses — even the names
are beautiful!) that is in the world.*

For some reason, I think here of my grandmother Jessie's house in Kirriemuir,

*Scotland. When I was a child growing up in Edinburgh, I visited her each sum-
mer. She had a lovely old stone house called "Roselea Cottage," and I always
remember the lavender that grew around the walk to the house. I would take some
home with me at the end of summer and make it into little cachets and, oh, the
scent was lovely! And that way, you see, I could have Grandmother Jessie with me
all year long!*

I read these words for the first time sitting in a rocking chair, surrounded by packing crates in my mother's apartment, a month after her
death from cancer in March 1985. I tried to picture her face as I read the
words but couldn't. Or, to put it more accurately, *wouldn't.* The tie was
still too powerful, the memories of the last two months, as she lay dying
in the hospital, still too painful, the sense of loss still too great. I closed
her book wondering if I would ever feel healed enough to open it again.

But in matters of healing — or *not* healing — the unconscious seems
to have its own clock and its own agenda. On a rainy Sunday afternoon
exactly one year from the day my mother entered the hospital, I suddenly
knew, in the most compelling way, that the time had come to remember
and honor her life — and her death. I knew also that it was time to
make my peace, if I could, with the loss of the most important influence
in my life.

And so the process began. For a full month, I pored over the daily
notebook I had kept during her hospitalization, the medical records I had
copied and carefully put away and, of course, my mother's book. I had no
idea what I was looking for or how any of this might help me.

And at first it didn't. More than once I found myself wondering if I
had simply unlocked a door behind which there was only more pain.

But when I was finished, I realized that something crucial had happened: My mother was no longer lost to me; in some new and different
way, I had regained her.

My mother's cancer was diagnosed three days after Christmas 1984,
when two tumors she accidentally discovered were biopsied and found to
be malignant. Wildly malignant, in fact — although such a phrase may be
redundant. By the time she went into the hospital a week later, it was the

end of the beginning of her illness and the beginning of the end of her life.

From my notes, dated Jan. 21, 1985:

My mother continues to amaze me. Despite the private realities of what is happening to her body — the disease is progressing with hatchet-like precision, cutting off one function after another, a new loss every day — she continues to appreciate nature and the small bits of life she can observe from her window in Room 235. There is a large evergreen magnolia framed by her window, and she seems to enjoy watching the birds busily flying in and out of it. "Look!" she said earlier today, pointing to the window. I looked just in time to see a beautiful red bird sail by, a scarlet arrow piercing the cloudless blue sky.

Her pain is awesome; she can no longer even sit up, but she is as interested as ever in what is happening outside her hospital room. Today is her grandson's birthday and somehow she managed to tear a page out of her address book and write a note to him. In it she reminded him of their mutual love of nature: "Hope you had a nice camping trip — how wonderful it is to enjoy the outdoor life." She also apologized — twice — for the erratic quality of her handwriting. Some day I will tell him of the unimaginable amount of effort his grandmother put into the physical act of writing this note.

As the days went by and it became clear that her illness was going to be a devastating one, my mother agreed, reluctantly, to see a psychoanalyst — an acquaintance of mine — who had a great deal of experience in working with terminally ill cancer patients. I stood by apprehensively as my mother — a woman who had never considered seeing a psychiatrist in her entire life — met Dr. Nathan Schnaper for the first time.

He introduced himself: "I'm Dr. Schnaper."

My mother's response was immediate: "What's your tartan?"

"MacSchnaper," he replied, without missing a beat.

My mother laughed. It was the start of a relationship that would become immeasurably important to her over the next six weeks as she grappled with the anger, depression, pain and, finally, acceptance of what was happening to her.

One of the things I remember most vividly about those last two

283

months was how chaotic the weather was — bitterly cold in January and then a February with temperatures so balmy — 84 degrees one day — that it actually forced out some blooms on an old azalea plant in my garden.

On one of those warm days — a day when the smell of the earth seemed to rise up to meet you, promising all sorts of things — I cracked open the window in her room. The soft, scented air spilled in, causing my mother to open her eyes and ask: "Is the grass beginning to grow?"

It was a private joke between us. I closed my eyes and a memory ran across the years to meet me:

I am about five-years-old and have crept out of the house in the middle of a warm summer night to watch the grass and flowers in our garden grow. Suddenly my mother is there at my side and instead of laughing at me and sending me back to bed, she joins me in my watch. I have never been up so late before and the sense of adventure is high. We sit there together in white, wooden lawn chairs that tilt back, listening to the cicadas making whirring noises in the trees and watch our cats — so cozy and domestic during the day — suddenly turn into night predators, stalking something through the long grass of the garden.

"Look," she says suddenly, pointing to a shooting star. But I am looking at the light in her eyes and her long, black hair, which is a spill of ink against the approaching dawn. Later I fall asleep with my head in her lap.

I opened my eyes and looked at my mother; she was in that half-sleep so typical of patients on heavy doses of painkillers. For the first time in a while, she looked like herself to me.

Sometimes a person faces dying in such a way as to give her life — and all that went before — a deeper, sharper meaning. It seemed to me that my mother's self-respect throughout her illness shielded her family from despair. At first such a lesson in courage only seems to make the loss more poignant, the grief less bearable.

I remember the day my mother asked that I write down a last message from her to each member of the family. "It will make them feel better," she told me, "if they can have a message from me after I die."

I wrote through my tears, aware that while my mother, with Dr.

Schnaper's help, had accepted her impending death, I hadn't. I was still trying to arrange for wheelchairs and walkers, trying to figure out how to get her on her feet again, how to get her home again. She saw my struggle and, as usual, waited for me to catch up with her.

I recall with extreme clarity the night I broke through my denial. From my notes — Jan. 26, 1985:

The radiation treatments, combined with the painkillers, are finally beginning to give her some relief. But the X-rays done earlier this week to try to pinpoint what is causing the paralysis of her left side were not so successful in terms of offering treatment options. She has been placed on a special motorized bed which moves constantly, the point being to try to take the pressure off specific parts of the body and alleviate the pain. Her vision is deteriorating in one eye; the other eye seems all right — for now.

Slowly I am giving up hope that any of the damage caused by her advancing illness can be reversed, that my mother will ever be the way she was. I think my mother is going to die.

I left the hospital that night at a low point. At home, I wandered from room to room and smashed the walls with my fists, unable to express my grief and rage in any other way. "A mother is not to lean on," she used to tell me, "but someone who makes leaning unnecessary." That advice seemed so distant to me now; I wanted *my* mother to lean on, and remembering the cruel perfection of the past did not help.

But *something* helped, because over the next few days I found I was able to discern more clearly what my mother wanted — *needed* — to do: She wanted to talk about her life; to hold the past like a globe and spin it round until all her memories were allowed to come into full view.

And so we began our long, final conversation. *Do you remember the time when ... Yes, yes, but do you remember what happened after that ... No, I'd forgotten that ...*

Back and forth we went, adding new pieces to the puzzle of memory until, finally, a picture of a life began to emerge from the stories that spilled out. And it seemed to me that as we talked and the picture of my mother's life grew stronger, so did she. Not in any physical way, of course,

285

but in a way that had to do with her being a *person* and not just a *patient* — old and sick and dying.

It was during one of these talks that I asked my mother if I could write about her, about her struggle and her courage. I needed to know if such an undertaking would be an invasion of her privacy.

She smiled wryly, and in that smile my old, familiar mother broke through the dark veil of illness that had been obscuring her: "And just what good are you as a writer," she asked, "if you *don't* write about what you see and feel?"

From my mother's book:

I haven't forgotten what it's like to be young — all of the hopes and anxieties you feel and the overwhelming sensation that everything you do, no matter how trivial, is going to advance or wreck your life. No in-betweens when you're young.

When I was young, my ambition was to go on the stage! And even though my father was very, very strict and taught his children to value discipline and education above all else, I managed — on the sly — to take elocution lessons and later formed a secret elocution club in the house on Great Western Road. My sister and I were allowed, however, to take lessons from a specialist in Scottish dances and we would go home to our lovely house with its large rooms, a fire aglow in each fireplace, and practice the intricate steps holding onto the back of a chair. I still recall them! In those days I thought I'd be a famous actress! It was all a dream, of course.

Lying in Room 235, my mother had other sorts of dreams. I remember a morning when she awoke in an agitated state, convinced that she had just seen a man fall from the roof of the hospital. All that day her thoughts were of falling. "Would I catch her when she fell?" she asked me over and over again, her voice anxious like that of a child who'd lost her way and needs help in finding the road back.

"Don't be afraid," I reassured her. "Of course I'll catch you. All those years when I was growing up, you caught me. Now it's my turn."

Her face relaxed under the oxygen mask and she closed her eyes.

I looked away, thinking: *For as long as I can, I will catch you. For as long as I can.*

But I knew there would come a time — and soon — when I would have to let go.

And so would she.

From my notes, February 23, 1985:

This has been a bad day from start to finish. There are problems with her breathing, problems with the IV, and she is suffering from intense pain that is difficult to control. Her face is ashen and there are dark circles of suffering around her eyes. And yet, despite all this, I saw my mother smile beneath the oxygen mask when I told her nurse the story of my mother and Max, my cat; of how my mother sat trapped in a lawn chair one spring afternoon for two hours because Max was napping on her lap and she didn't want to disturb him.

I don't know whether to feel happy or sad about her smile: happy because it offers hope that her connection to life is still there; or sad because it only heightens the sense of all that is being lost here in this hospital room.

There were days when the strong drugs she was taking caused my mother to hallucinate. I was extremely frightened each time this happened, fearing that her lucidity would never return, that she had gone permanently to a place where I could not follow.

But somehow — with a change of medicine and the reassuring presence of Dr. Schnaper, who spoke with her once, sometimes twice, a day — she kept fighting her way back to reality.

From medical notes, February 25, signed by Dr. Schnaper:

Patient weaker every day. Physically more incapacitated but mentally not depressed — more accepting.

But accepting the inevitability of death, it seems, does not make it any less difficult to let go of life.

Five days before she died — on a particularly beautiful winter day — we watched in silence as the late afternoon light glanced the side of a red brick building opposite her window. The wind was tossing around the branches of a young beech tree while the sun silvered the promising red buds that already swelled with life at the tip of each branch.

"Close the curtains," she said suddenly, looking away sadly from the beauty which seemed both insolent and innocent in its indifference to her suffering. She sighed and closed her eyes, retreating from the play of light and life that was not her world anymore.

Months later, I would gaze into the eye of a dying bird that had crash-landed in my garden and be reminded of the look on her face that day.

Without knowing why, I began taking home her clothes that night. From my notes, March 1, 1985:

She is very, very weak today and her breathing is quite labored and irregular. But her spirit is still connected to nature, to the world. When I held the pot of jonquils close to her bed to show her the new, pale yellow bloom bursting out, she said — with genuine delight in her voice — "Oh, that's so pretty! Isn't it wonderful how life goes on?"

She wanted to talk about her family, especially her grandchildren. "Don't let anything happen to their characters," she told me over and over again, pausing between each reminiscence to emphasize this.

Looking back at that next-to-last day of my mother's life, I have wondered more than once whether it was coincidence — or something else — that caused one of her grandsons to leave school suddenly and to show up at her bedside only hours before she veered away from life, lapsing into her final coma.

She had been hearing music for the last few days, she told him when he arrived. A choir singing. *Do you hear it?* she asked him, straining forward. *Do you hear the music?* Her grandson walked around to the side of the bed and gently lowered his head next to hers, listening in silence. Then he straightened up: "I think I hear it too," he said evenly, his fine, clear eyes filled with the life-light that was slowly fading from hers.

She seemed pleased that someone else heard the music and appeared to doze off. For the rest of the afternoon, she wavered between consciousness and disorientation. At 5:30 p.m., Dr. Schnaper came to see her. "Thank you for all you've done," she said as he leaned over to kiss her goodbye.

As it grew dark outside, I saw my mother staring out the window into the blackness. "What are you looking at?" I asked her. "Nothing," she replied. "Well," I said, "how about looking at *me*?"

More than anything else, I wanted her last conscious moments to be spent looking at the face of someone who loved her.

About a month after my mother died, I planted a garden in her memory. It seemed to me then, as it does now, the way in which I could remain closest to her spirit. There are some flowers in this garden, but mostly it's planted with things that will grow and change and deepen in beauty over the years: mountain laurel, a weeping Japanese maple, azaleas, juniper, winterberry, and a graceful Kousa dogwood whose white, star-shaped blossoms appear in early June.

Once last summer, when the first brilliant yellow lily appeared at the end of its impossibly long, swaying, green stem, I ran into the house to telephone my mother with the news. Then I remembered.

Even now, a year later, I keep forgetting she is dead; I keep thinking of things I ought to tell her, things I want to ask her. She had a way of giving perspective to my life; of reminding me that I was building my life on the foundation of those who had come before me and that it was my duty to give that past to my children for their future.

From my mother's book:

Growing old is not at all the way you think it's going to be. When I turned 70, someone asked me how it felt to have arrived at such an age. Well, even though my body isn't the same, I am still the same. I will always be the girl who loved cats and flowers and raced home from school to practice my dancing lessons. Inside I am still that person.

I miss that person. ⊕

289

Homer:
A Dog's Odyssey

The signs went up in the neighborhood two weeks ago: "Lost Dog. Female Golden Retriever. 6 Months Old. Very Sweet. Family Heartsick. Reward."

One of the signs was posted outside the supermarket, and as I stopped to read it, a woman I didn't know also paused to look at it.

"That's so sad," she said. "I sure hope they get her back. I remember when I was a little girl and Ginger got lost. I cried for a month."

"I know what you mean," I said. "When Homer disappeared, I searched for him for six months. And dreamed about him for a year."

Then something funny happened: Standing there on that busy sidewalk, cars whizzing by, suddenly it seemed as though the ghosts of dogs past began to rise up and hover in the air above. It was like being in one of those Chagall paintings where flowers or people are always surrealistically floating above whatever reality exists below.

I mean, I hadn't thought about Homer for years. Decades, actually.

But now, here I was remembering the day my mother officially declared Homer lost and suggested we compose an ad for the newspaper.

I don't remember the exact wording of the ad, of course, but I do remember the effort I put into describing Homer accurately. It was something along the lines of: "Tall, good-looking, incredibly friendly, part-Labrador, part-German shepherd, brownish-golden. Answers to name of Homer. Also answers to Pee Wee and Laddie Boy. Is probably hungry."

It's funny, but descriptions given by owners of pets are seldom realistic. It's one of the things I learned while writing an article about the SPCA. I recall, for instance, when a cat owner came in to see if anyone had turned in a "silver gray cat with violet-colored eyes." The person took a look around, then spotted this scruffy, oil-colored cat with light, watery eyes and screamed: "Elizabeth, it's you!"

The point I'm making is that maybe Homer wasn't brownish-golden, but brown. And maybe he wasn't as tall as I remember. But he *was* friendly. And maybe he wasn't actually the best-looking dog in the neighborhood. But he was always hungry.

In fact, I guess my first memory of Homer has to do with eating. He was a stray dog — and a hungry one — when my father brought him home on a hot summer day. He'd found the dog, lean as a bone, hanging around the garage where the family Plymouth was being readied for a trip to the Mohawk Trail.

By the time the two of them got home, my father had already named the dog Homer. It was a tribute, he told us, to a man who wrote a story about a sailor who wandered the seas, searching for his way home.

As it turned out, our Homer's wandering days were over. He fit into our lives just fine. Of course, he worked at it. There were certain duties, for instance, that he took on as his own. Protecting me from the bully in the next block was one. And walking me home from school was another.

See, that's what dogs did then. In fact, most afternoons at about 2:45, the neighborhood dogs would gather on the school playground. I remember looking through the window of Mrs. Stanhope's third-grade class and seeing them scattered around; some in half-sprawls, some in sphinx-like positions, and a few rolling around in the soft, red dirt of the

291

softball field. Homer usually fell into this last category.

But this familiar routine was broken one night when Homer didn't respond to the kitchen-door cries of: "Here Homer, here doggie, here boy."

Things started getting tense the next night. We began walking the neighborhood alleys calling out "Homer, Homer, Pee Wee, Laddie Boy." We looked in his favorite spots and drove the car as far away as the York Road Steak House, a place where Homer had once been led by his acute sense of smell.

On the fourth day, my mother said: Write the ad.

The ad produced some possible Homer-sightings. A couple of times we got our hopes up, but arrived at the caller's home to find that Homer was not the only lost dog.

Once, I remember our hopes soared when a neighbor spotted a Homer look-alike near Darnell's Grocery Store. But it turned out to be a neighbor's new dog.

For months we kept alive the hope that Homer would return. Every morning I checked the furrow beneath the backyard hedges — the one shaped just like Homer's curled body — to see if he was there. And I looked for him out the classroom window, oh, I guess, for six months or so.

My recurring dream lasted longer — for about a year. In the dream, Homer was cast as a rogue-dog buccaneer sailing the high seas. He even had a black patch over one of his eyes.

I'm embarrassed to admit it — although only a little embarrassed — but I still picture him that way. ⊕

Elegy for Max

I f I had to describe Max in just one word, it would be questing. Max was definitely a questing kind of cat.

He was always searching for something. And, unlike some cats I know, he pursued each day with a singular sense of adventuresome purpose.

Sometimes Max's quest took him away from home for a few days. But always when he returned from the road, you knew from his demeanor that this was a cat who had done what he had set out to do. After such trips, but before setting out on his next adventure, Max liked to spend a few days sleeping.

Of course, he never had to look that far for excitement. Momentous things occurred in Max's life every day. The sun rose each morning. Birds flew overhead in Max's sky, and squirrels chattered in his trees. There were backyards to be explored and trees to be climbed. There were basement doors to dart inside and furnace rooms to explore.

And, naturally, given Max's penchant for exploration, there'd be close calls, too. Getting stuck in an attic crawl space, for instance. Or being locked in a neighbor's garage for a weekend.

But such is the fate of the questing cat: it leads a life filled with risk. But satisfaction, too.

Which reminds me: For all the satisfaction Max got out of his exhausting, questing schedule, he also believed in kicking back and relaxing on a regular basis.

One of the things he most loved to do during his off-duty hours was to fish. Often in the spring, I would see Max stretched out in the sun, fishing from the side of a neighbor's pond. Leisurely — he wasn't a serious fishercat — he'd rake his paw through the water, aiming at the little golden darts that flashed just beneath the surface.

And in the summer, Max loved to sleep in the sun. His favorite spot was in the middle of the tall, swaying day lilies whose color — orange — perfectly complemented his own orange and white spots. From my bedroom window, I would spot him sleeping there, his heart-shaped face parting the flowers directly in front of him.

A lot of people thought Max was haughty. But I saw him as a cat who was particularly adept at putting his paw on whatever was irrelevant to his lifestyle. He paid no attention, for instance, to suggestions that he not sleep in the linen closet, or that he not use a silk chair as his scratching post. He turned aside such suggestions with something approaching disdain.

Somehow I always imagined that if Max were a person, he'd be a lot like James Thurber: witty and urbane, with a sharp eye for the ridiculous.

Max was afraid of nothing. As a result, he ruled the neighborhood. Cat-wise, that is. Most of the "catz 'n the hood" went out of their way to stay out of his path. Not that he was mean. But the blood of imperial Egyptian cats flowed in Max, and he ruled accordingly.

Max came to us as a stray kitten 16 years ago. Just showed up in the backyard one evening and never left. For 16 years he was my faithful companion and the friend of my children's youth. And to the end, despite his age and illness, he retained all the qualities that added up to Max.

The end came last weekend. It seems fitting that Max's departure from this earth coincided with the arrival of a blizzard. In fact, the sight of all that snow briefly revived Max's questing instinct.

For the first time in months, Max wanted to go outside. And I wanted him to go outside, too. I wanted Max to feel the crunch of snow under his paws one more time. I wanted him to smell the alpine freshness of the winter air and to see a blue jay flash against the high, cold sky one more time.

And because I knew this was to be his last day on earth, there was something I wanted to see one more time: his footprints in the snow.

Outside, a break in the overcast skies threw a wide slant of sunlight against the back porch, and I watched Max position himself in the center of it.

Max always liked to be at the center of things.

Later that night, when the vet came to ease Max into his final sleep, I noticed he was purring. It was the last sound he made.

The next morning I got up early and went out to see if Max's footprints were still visible in the snow. They were.

For some reason, I thought of how in springtime I used to love to smell the scent of the damp, fertile earth on those paws. It was like smelling life itself.

And then I remembered something about how life works. I remembered how, beneath all the snow, the jonquils were blooming.   ⊕

Empty Nest

Inside my house they were drinking champagne and toasting the two young men who were about to set off on separate journeys: One was leaving to spend a year in Japan after graduating from college; the other was off to Colorado to climb mountains before returning to postgraduate academic life.

It was a happy occasion — my two sons about to turn important corners in their young lives — but inside my head, mixed with the happiness, I thought I heard the distant rumble of sadness. It was a feeling of loss, I guess; an empty feeling that seemed to be gathering itself together in a dangerous pattern, like a summer tornado.

The room was filled with young people talking of the dreams they planned to carve out of the future; assessing the rough material of their lives like sculptors sizing up the stone slab from which a finished figure would emerge. As this one talked of graduate school in Boston and that one of a job in New Zealand, the air was resonant with the sound of doors opening.

But it was the faint sound of other doors closing that drove me, briefly, out from the celebration and into my garden.

Outside, the wind had come up suddenly and the evening sky was turning a sullen gray. The old, orange-and-white cat — a fixture of my children's youth — stirred himself from his sphinxlike pose beneath the huge azalea bushes. I noticed how overgrown the old azaleas suddenly seemed — I reckoned them to be about 50 years old — and how, weighted down with all those years of growing and blooming, they looked tired somehow, in need of a new start.

As I wandered back inside, I told myself that once the sons were gone, I would cut back the old azaleas. It would be risky. I knew that. There was no guarantee they would survive the kind of pruning I had in mind. But maybe it was time to take the risk.

The sadness didn't let up during the following week as both sons prepared to move on. I found myself assigning the largest significance to even the smallest gesture; each routine act now embodied the concept of The Last Time:

This is the last time I'll see the younger son holding the old cat on his lap, I thought, observing the two of them in the garden.

This is the last time the older son will sit in my room and talk to me about my work. "How's it going down there at the newspaper?" he'd ask. "Are you happy?"

And this is the last time the three of us will stand in the kitchen cooking dinner together.

Changes. Why do they always feel like endings to me? I remember the sadness I felt when it was time for my sons to enter school, or go off to summer camp and, later, college. Despite the satisfaction I derived from their growing mastery of the world, the sadness always hovered. Why?

Oddly enough, I ran across a helpful thought while leafing through an old notebook. Scribbled there next to the name of artist Jackson Pollock was this observation on the act of painting: "There is no form we cannot associate with another form; something is always like something else."

I guess that can be true of emotions too. It seems I'm always associating one emotion with another. And more to the point, I'm unconsciously *mistaking* one emotion for the other. Change, I had to remind myself, is not the equivalent of loss. And while the process of maturation may change the form that's visible, it does not destroy the old shape underneath; that remains the framework for all that follows.

And you know what? Once I started looking at my sons with this kind of X-ray vision, things got better. Because I found that the young boys I was having trouble saying goodbye to still existed underneath the young men who were moving on. And what a relief it was to find them again! I reasoned that, if I could find them once, I could find them as often as I needed to.

It made me think of the time when I was in my 30s and returned to my mother's house as a weekend guest. There I was, back in my childhood room with its familiar maple bed. I went to sleep listening to my old, white Motorola radio and woke up to the smell of Scottish scones baking. By the second morning, it seemed like I had never left.

And, in a way, I hadn't. It was Me who woke up in that room as a child. And it was Me who woke up there as an adult. The years and the memories had knit the two together — child and adult — without my even knowing it.

In the coming weeks, the cat and I will try to remember that. ⊕

Remembering E.B. White

He was the *New Yorker's* quintessential writer and a man responsible for some of the most graceful, elegant prose ever written. But when it came to describing how he felt about the death of Fred, his beloved and egocentric dachshund, E.B. White just gave it to us straight: "He's dead, damn it. I would feel a lot better this morning if I could just see Fred's face … He was something."

Now, damn it, E.B. White is dead. He died yesterday at age 86 in North Brooklyn, Maine, where he had lived for the last 45 years. He was something, all right, and it's going to be difficult to get used to the idea that the man who gave us "Charlotte's Web," "Stuart Little," and a collection of near-perfect essays won't be around to remind us, in his wry, optimistic way, that the small, commonplace moment often illuminates the larger, valuable truth.

Whether writing about the emotional perils of opening a box of old letters stored in the attic, or the folly of owning a tempestuous dachshund, or the dizzying, eerie feeling evoked on a late Sunday morning, E.B. White saw things with a unique eye and then, through the sensibility of the self he once referred to as "a boy I knew," fashioned a lasting view of the world.

How, for instance, are we supposed to accept the silence of a voice that tells us this about an adult's return trip to a boyhood vacation spot: "It is strange how much you can remember about places like that once you allow your mind to return into the grooves that lead back. You remember one thing and that suddenly reminds you of another thing. I guess I remembered clearest of all the early mornings when the lake was cool and motionless, remembered how the bedroom smelled of the lumber it was made of and of the wet woods whose scent entered through the screen."

At the heart of all of E.B. White's writing was his willingness to let the adult man step aside and the boy who resided within to remember. And always, it seems, the boy — and the man — responded with remembered love and wonder to the world around them. To a reader of "Charlotte's Web" — that incomparable story of true friendship between a pig and a spider — White once wrote: "All that I hope to say in books, all that I ever hope to say, is that I love the world. I guess you can find that in there, if you dig around."

You don't have to dig very far to turn up the love he felt for nature and animals. Here he is, for instance, writing from his farm in Maine about the death of a pig (at age 39, White left New York city and the staff of the *New Yorker*, where he was the star, to move to the country): "At intervals during the last day, I took cool fresh water down to him [the pig] and, at such times as he found the strength to get to his feet, he would stand with his head in the pail and snuffle his snout around. ... Once, near the last, while I was attending him, I saw him try to make a bed for himself, but he lacked the strength, and when he set his snout into the dust, he was unable to plow even the little furrow he needed to lie down in.

"... I went back up to the house and to bed, and cried internally — deep hemorrhagic intears. I didn't wake till nearly eight the next morning, and when I looked out the open window, the grave was already being dug. ... I could hear the spade strike against the small rocks that blocked the way. Never send to know for whom the grave is dug, I said to myself, it's dug for thee."

It was precisely this kind of writing that prompted E.B. White's dear friend, humorist James Thurber, to describe White as one who "understands begonias and children, canaries and goldfish, dachshunds and Scottish terriers, men and motives. His ear not only notes the louder cosmic rhythms, but the faint ticking sounds."

White's own explanation of how he spun out his gossamer, shimmering essays is characteristically modest and slightly bemused: "The truth is I write by ear, always with difficulty, and seldom with any exact knowledge of what is taking place under the hood," he wrote in a 1959 preface to "The Elements of Style," a respected and compact guidebook for writers which he co-authored with William Strunk, Jr.

But if he pleaded little knowledge of *how* he wrote, *why* he wrote was as clear and lucid to him as one of his essays. He supplies us the reason in a letter to an older brother written at age 47, some eight years after the break from city life: "... even now, at this late date, a blank sheet of paper holds the greatest excitement there is for me. ... It holds all the hope there is, all fears. I can remember, really quite distinctly, looking a sheet of paper square in the eyes when I was seven or eight-years-old and thinking 'This is where I belong, this is it.'"

He also belonged to Maine, in the end never regretting his decision to move from the heady New York literary life to the country: "Once in everyone's life there is apt to be a period when he is fully awake, instead of half asleep. I think of those ... years in Maine as the time when this happened to me. ... I was suddenly seeing, feeling, and listening as a child sees, feels, and listens."

More than 30 years ago, E.B. White, who was known to be a bit of a hypochondriac, wrote a premature farewell of sorts: "A man who is over fifty, as am I, is sure that he has only about twenty minutes to live, and it is natural, I suppose, that he should feel disposed to put his affairs in order, such as they are, to harvest what fruit he has not already picked up

301

and stored away against the winter, and to tie his love for the world into a convenient bundle, accessible to all."

White, of course, had a habit of recording his farewells. Over the years, he said his goodbyes to his dachshund, Fred; to the Model-T; to New York and the high, literary life he lived there; to a sky that has stars instead of space debris and satellites; to his wife, Katharine; and to dear friends.

One of those dear friends was Harold Ross, the legendary editor of the *New Yorker* and a man, apparently, who knew the value of White's presence on the magazine's staff. One day, after reading something of White's that pleased him, Ross left a simple note on his star writer's desk: "I am encouraged to go on."

E. B. White is gone now, but the remarkable body of work he leaves behind — so full of grace and beauty and clarity — encourages all of us to go on. ⊕

The Girl Who Loved the Wind

T he first year was the hardest.

Even now, six years later, I can remember with amazing clarity waking up that Sunday morning, two months after my mother's death, and thinking:

Today is Mother's Day. And for the first time in my life I will spend this day as a motherless child.

It was a mournful thought, one that played over and over in my head like a dirge. But since I was a mother as well as a daughter, I put aside my sadness, or tried to, in order to concentrate on the Mother's Day surprises my sons had planned for me.

But when I was alone that night — the night of my first Mother's Day without a mother — I found myself sitting under a small circle of light in my bedroom, rereading parts of "Jane Eyre."

I was drawn particularly to the part where the orphaned, 10-year-old Jane is transported late one night by carriage to Lowood School and, with no preparation, is set down abruptly into the fearful, unprotected world of the parentless child. As she steps out of the carriage, young Jane is approached by the headmistress of Lowood, and the immense impersonality of her greeting to this abandoned girl sent sharp pangs of grief through me:

"'Is there a little girl called Jane Eyre here?' she asked. I answered 'Yes,' and was then lifted out; my trunk was handed down, and the coach instantly drove away.'"

I think I sobbed out loud at that point, and I would not be offended if you thought my outburst silly. After all, there I was, a grown woman with two teen-age sons, crying over a fictional orphan girl. But sitting there in the middle of the night, alone and wrapped in a quilt, the house around me silent and sleeping, the grown woman was scarcely present at all: It was the child within me who sobbed bitterly, feeling suddenly abandoned and set down, as Jane Eyre had been, in the alien world of the motherless child.

Someone once said that there are no such things as adults; that there are only children who try — usually without success — to *imitate* adults. However, what I found out that Mother's Day night six years ago was this: There is but one response to the death of a mother, no matter your age. What the child feels in the face of this loss is what the adult feels. The difference lies in the way such emotions are civilized by the adult into more socially acceptable grieving.

For child or adult, it seems to me the task created by a mother's death remains the same: Suddenly your world has heaved and shifted, creating an emotional fault line that alters the underlying structure of your life — and suddenly you've got to find your place in the world again. A new place.

But how difficult it is to move on and give up the old, familiar place! For one thing, it is the homeland of your childhood; the place where things get etched into you in a way that never happens again. Six years have passed since my mother's death and still it all comes back to me, sometimes, in a rush of memory as clear as the water in a mountain lake — exactly how she looked and what she said and precisely what I felt looking at her and listening to her.

She loved the wind.

When I was growing up, my mother would often recite this poem to my brother and me:

"Who has seen the wind?
Neither you nor I,
But when the trees bow down their heads,
The wind is passing by."

She told me once about how, when she was a little girl walking to church, the wind lifted her hat off her head and carried it down to the bottom of a steep incline. It was her best hat — navy straw with a white grosgrain band around the brim — and she was afraid she'd be scolded for losing it. So, dressed in her Sunday best, she climbed down, through the underbrush, to the bottom of the hill to retrieve it. Which she did — along with an abandoned kitten who was to become my mother's most beloved childhood pet. She named him Zephyr, she told me, because he was as light as a gentle breeze.

In the family album, there's an old photograph of Zephyr and my mother. In it, my mother — who must have been about 10 at the time — is standing in the garden behind the house where she grew up, holding a small, gray cat who's struggling to jump out of her arms. The motion blurred Zephyr's tail, causing it to look in the picture like a huge, gray, floating feather.

Looking at the photo recently, I tried to imagine what the girl who would become my mother was feeling at that very moment, as she smiled into the camera lens. I noticed that the wind was blowing a few loose strands of her long, dark hair across her eyes. Did she smile perhaps — this girl who loved the wind — at the feel of the breeze touching her face? Or did the cat's predictable struggle to escape evoke in her, as it always does in me, the wish to laugh at the way cats will never do what you want them to do?

It's odd, but in the six years since her death, I've thought more and

305

more of the child revealed to me in my mother's stories about herself, and less and less of the adult woman I actually knew.

For instance, she told me that as a little girl she loved dogs but was not allowed to have one because of her brother's fear of them. But she yearned for a puppy so much that finally she decided an imaginary canine pet was in order. So she invented one: A spotted, medium-sized, bloodhound-type dog. She gave him a name — Morley — and every night before going to bed she would go to the back door and call him in.

Usually at this point, my mother would begin acting out the story. I can picture it even now, as I write these words: My mother suddenly becoming a little girl in a long nightgown, her black hair in a braid falling to her waist, standing at the door on a frosty, winter night calling out into the dark to her imaginary dog, her breath forming little clouds in the cold air: "Morley. Morley. Here, Morley."

Funny, but as I grow older, the child my mother was seems to follow me about more and more.

Recently, for example, I was standing downtown near the harbor when the unexpected sound of bagpipes floated across the water. Immediately I pictured my mother as a young girl growing up in Scotland, practicing the intricate dance steps of the Highland fling in front of a mirror. The thought made me smile. And then it occurred to me it was exactly the way a parent smiles at a happy memory connected to a daughter or son.

I guess you could say that this additional way of seeing my mother — as my child, so to speak — is one of the things that's helped me find my new place in the world.

In the first years after she died, I wanted to keep my mother alive, keep her a person and not a memory. But this, I found, was not possible. And while I have not forgotten that I am the daughter of a woman who, when old and dying, could still comment on the beauty of the jonquils, the discovery of the child within my mother links me to her in ways stronger than before.

Still, every once in a while, something will happen to me — usually something nice or something troubling — and I find myself picking up the phone to call her. Sometimes, memories aren't enough.

I saw the future the other night. It happened while I was drinking tea in the kitchen, stirring it with a silver spoon that had been my mother's. I thought of her, remembered the way she would hand me the silverware each night when it was time to set the dinner table.

And suddenly it occurred to me, standing there in the silence of my kitchen: Someday, one of my sons will be doing something, standing somewhere, in a flower store perhaps, amid the scent of roses — which I love — and he'll think of me in a rush of memory just as I now think of her.

But that lies in my son's future. Not mine.

I opened the kitchen door. A breeze blew in carrying the scent of hyacinth. You've been six years out of the wind, I thought. Then I found myself saying, to no one in particular:

"Who has seen the wind?
Neither you nor I,
But when the trees bow down their heads,
The wind is passing by." ⊕

About the Author

Alice Steinbach, a journalist since 1977, has been a reporter, feature writer, and columnist for the Baltimore Sun since 1981. In 1985, she won the Pulitzer Prize for Feature Writing. In the years since, she has won many major journalism awards for both her reporting and her column, which ran from 1989 through 1993. Her work, which features a literary style of journalism, is distributed nationally on the Los Angeles Times-Washington Post wire service.

Steinbach, along with Anna Quindlen and Molly Ivins, is one of nine women journalists featured in "Women on Deadline: A Collection of America's Best" (Iowa State University Press, 1993). Her work has also appeared in several other books on journalism: "The Complete Book of Feature Writing" (Writer's Digest Books, 1991); "Writing: Strategies for All Disciplines" (Prentice Hall, 1985); and "Feature Writing for Newspapers and Magazines" (Harper Collins, 1993).

Steinbach did radio commentary for several years, as well as a call-in talk show, for WBAL-AM in Baltimore, MD. In 1994, she did twice-a-week television commentary for WJZ-TV in Baltimore.

Her work as a freelance journalist has appeared in many major magazines, including Glamour, McCalls, Redbook, Woman's Day, and Reader's Digest.

It has also appeared in The Washington Post, The Philadelphia Inquirer, San Francisco Examiner, Chicago Sun Times, Boston Globe, and many other newspapers around the country.

In 1991 and 1992, she taught a senior seminar in Creative Nonfiction Writing at Loyola College in Baltimore.

Steinbach lives in her native Baltimore. She has two grown sons.